The Latin Chronicle
of the Kings of Castile

Medieval and Renaissance Texts and Studies

Volume 236

The Latin Chronicle
of the Kings of Castile

Translated
with an Introduction and Notes
by

Joseph F. O'Callaghan

Arizona Center for Medieval and Renaissance Studies
Tempe, Arizona
2002

*The publication of this volume has been greatly assisted by
a grant from the Program for Cultural Cooperation between
Spain's Ministry of Culture and the United States Universities.*

Dust jacket image: The Effigy of Fernando III on his Tomb erected in
the Cathedral of Seville by his Son Alfonso X. *Cantigas de Santa Maria*, F 10 (E 292). Florence, Biblioteca Nazionale, MS Banco Rari 20.
By permission of Edilán-Ars Libri, Madrid.

Library of Congress Cataloging-in-Publication Data

Chronica latina regum Castellae. English.
 The Latin chronicle of the kings of Castile / translated with an
introduction and notes by Joseph F. O'Callaghan.
  p. cm. — (Medieval & Renaissance Texts & Studies (Series) ; v.
  236)
 Includes bibliographical references and index.
 ISBN 0-86698-278-7 (alk. paper)
 1. Castile (Spain)—History. I. O'Callaghan, Joseph F. II. Title.
III. Series.
DP134.8.C3713 2001
946'.3—dc21

                                                  2001022435

This book is made to last.
It is set in Bembo,
smythe-sewn and printed on acid-free paper
to library specifications.

Printed in the United States of America

For

Michael, Megan, Thomas
Rónán & Peter

Contents

The Latin Chronicle of the Kings of Castile

I. FROM COUNT FERNÁN GONZÁLEZ TO
KING SANCHO III (923–1158)

CONTENTS

CONTENTS

CONTENTS

Stemma 1

Kings of León, Castile, and Portugal
in the Eleventh, Twelfth, and Thirteenth Centuries

Sancho III of Navarre 1000–1035

Fernando I of León-Castile 1035–1065

Alfonso VI of León-Castile 1065–1109

Urraca of León-Castile 1109–1126 = (1) Raymond of Burgundy   Teresa = Henry of Burgundy

Afonso I Henriques of Portugal 1128–1185

Alfonso VII of León-Castile 1126–1157

Fernando II of León 1157–1188

Sancho I of Portugal 1185–1211

Sancho III of Castile 1157–1158

Alfonso VIII of Castile 1158–1214

Berenguela (2) = Alfonso IX of León = (1) Teresa 1188–1230

Afonso II of Portugal 1211–1223

Enrique I of Castile 1214–1217

Fernando III of Castile-León 1223–1248

Sancho II of Portugal 1217–1252

Stemma 2

THE KINGS OF ARAGÓN AND NAVARRE AND THE COUNTS OF BARCELONA

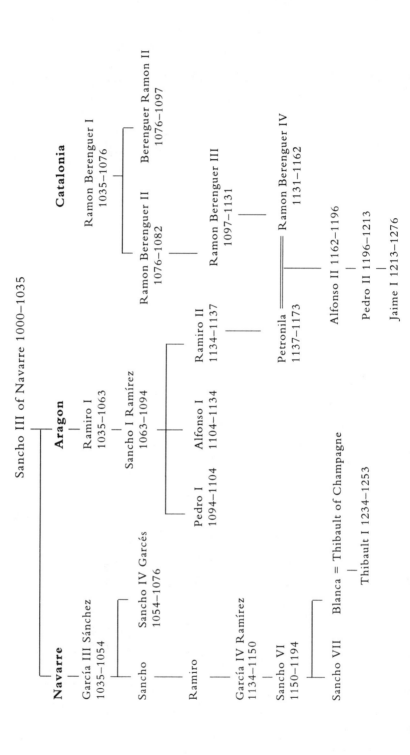

Stemma 3

THE ALMOHAD CALIPHS

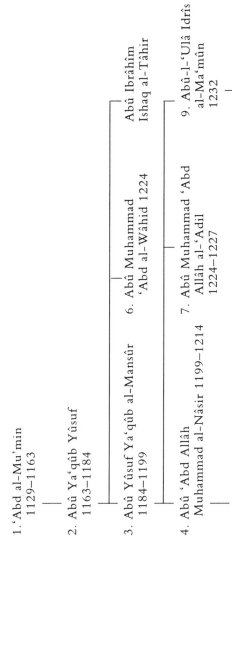

1. ʿAbd al-Muʾmin
   1129–1163

2. Abû Yaʿqûb Yûsuf
   1163–1184

3. Abû Yûsuf Yaʿqûb al-Mansûr
   1184–1199

4. Abû ʿAbd Allâh
   Muhammad al-Nâsir 1199–1214

5. Abû Yaʿqûb Yûsuf
   1214–1224

   Abû Ibrâhîm
   Ishaq al-Tâhir

6. Abû Muhammad
   ʿAbd al-Wâhid 1224

7. Abû Muhammad ʿAbd
   Allâh al-ʿAdil
   1224–1227

9. Abû-l-ʿUlâ Idrîs
   al-Maʾmûn
   1232

10. Abû Muhammad
    al-Wâhid al-Rashîd
    1242

8. Abû Zakariya' Yahyâ
   al-Muʿtasim
   1227–1229

11. Abû-l-Hasan ʿAlî
    al-Mustansir al-Saʿid
    1242–1248

12. Abû Hafs ʿUmar al-Murtadâ
    1248–1266

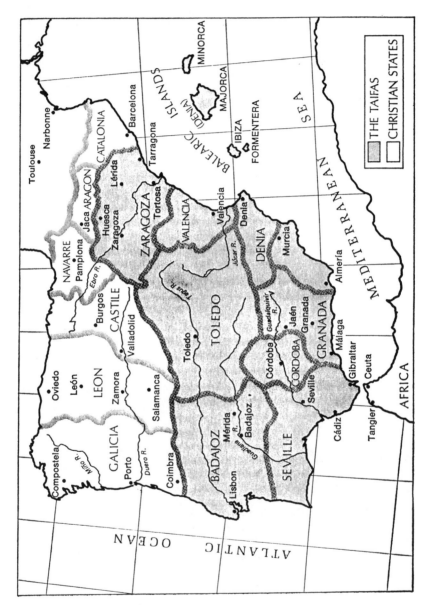

Spain at the Death of Fernando I, 1065

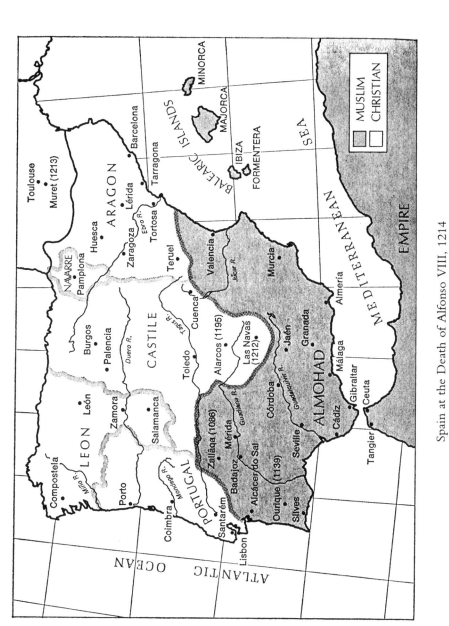

Spain at the Death of Alfonso VIII, 1214

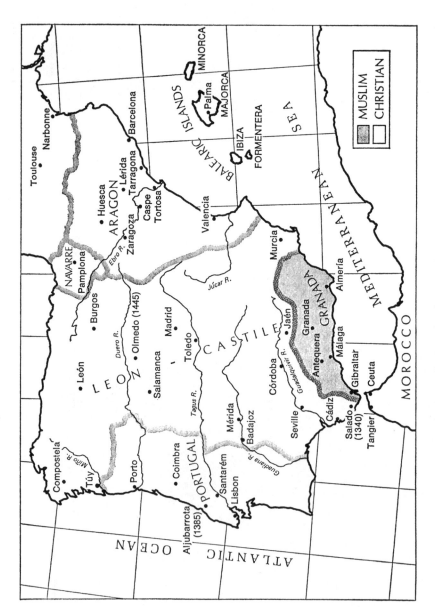

Spain at the Death of Fernando III, 1252

Preface

When I first offered a course in the history of medieval Spain to undergraduates at Fordham University more than forty years ago, I discovered that I had neither a textbook nor any collection of translated sources. As a consequence, I set out to remedy the situation by writing *A History of Medieval Spain*. I also translated some materials for use in my classes, and began a translation of *The Latin Chronicle of the Kings of Castile*. Other concerns distracted me from the latter task, which I took up again recently and finally completed. My purpose in translating this work is to provide undergraduates who have little or no knowledge of Latin with an early thirteenth-century account of the affairs of the kingdom of Castile during the reigns of Alfonso VIII (1158–1214) and Fernando III (1217–1252).

This was an important period in peninsular history because of the confrontation between Christian Spain and the Almohads, a Muslim sect from Morocco, who dominated Islamic Spain for nearly a century. The breakup of the Almohad empire enabled the Christian kings of Spain to conquer significant towns and their dependent territories. The *Latin Chronicle* relates the catastrophe of Alarcos in 1195, when Alfonso VIII was thoroughly routed by the Almohads, and his extraordinary triumph over them at Las Navas de Tolosa in 1212. Moreover, the author, who appears to be the royal chancellor Juan, bishop first of Osma and then of Burgos, comments in detail on Fernando III's campaigns against the Muslims, culminating in his conquest of Córdoba in 1236. At the same time the author speaks about extrapeninsular affairs such as the Albigensian Crusade, the Third and Fourth Crusades, and the Crusade of Emperor Frederick II and his subsequent conflict with the papacy. In effect, *The Latin Chronicle,* besides being a major source for peninsular development in the late twelfth and early thirteenth centuries, also offers a Castilian perspective on the wider world.

It is my hope that this translation will encourage students to inquire more deeply into the history of medieval Spain and that those whose attention has generally been focused on northern Europe will discover that events in the Iberian peninsula had a great significance not only in their own right but also for the general history of western Europe.

Professor Luis Charlo Brea of the University of Cádiz edited the *Chronicle* on two occasions and also translated it into Spanish, thereby greatly facilitating my labors; he also kindly provided me with an offprint of an important article bearing on the subject matter. To him I owe special thanks. I am also grateful to Dr. Robert Bjork and the readers who recommended this translation for publication in the series Medieval and Renaissance Texts and Studies. I especially wish to thank Dr. Leslie S. B. MacCoull for her careful reading of the translation and her many excellent suggestions. Dr. Karen Lemiski, production manager and publishing coordinator, and her staff were also most helpful.

I wish to thank in a special way Francisco Requena Sánchez and Edilán-Ars Libri for permission to use the cover illustration of Fernando III of Castile-Leon.

Introduction

The *Latin Chronicle of the Kings of Castile* is one of the three principal narrative sources for the history of the kingdoms of Castile and León written in the early thirteenth century. The *History of the Affairs of Spain (Historia de rebus Hispanie)* by Rodrigo Jiménez de Rada, Archbishop of Toledo (d. 1247), is a general history of Spain from antiquity to a few years after the fall of Córdoba in 1236; as such it established the framework on which the other later major historical works of medieval Spain were patterned.[1] Lucas, Bishop of Túy (d. 1249), in his book, the *Chronicle of the World (Chronicon mundi)*, set out to record the history of the world from creation, but for the most part limited himself chiefly to Spain from the earliest settlement down to the conquest of Córdoba.[2] Whereas Archbishop Rodrigo's history is distinguished by its elegant style, that of Bishop Lucas is noteworthy for the author's willingness to report any and every fantastic story. The *Latin Chronicle* is more limited in scope as the author concentrated his attention mainly on the history of the kingdom of Castile in the late twelfth and early thirteenth centuries.

Before describing the salient characteristics of the *Latin Chronicle*, an overview of peninsular history from the Muslim conquest in the eighth century

---

[1] Rodrigo Jiménez de Rada, *Historia de rebus Hispanie sive Historia Gothica*, ed. Juan Fernández Valverde, Corpus Christianorum Continuatio Mediaevalis 72 (Turnhout: Brepols, 1987). See also Benito Sánchez Alonso, *Historia de la historiografía española,* 2 vols. (Madrid: Consejo superior de Investigaciones científicas, 1941–1944) and idem, *Fuentes de la historia española e hispanoamericana,* 3d ed., 3 vols. (Madrid: Revista de Filología española, 1952).

[2] Lucas of Túy, *Chronicon mundi,* ed. Andreas Schott, *Hispania Illustrata,* 4 vols. (Frankfort: Claudius Marnius et Heredes Joannis Aubrii, 1603–1608), 4:1–116. The *Crónica de España,* ed. and trans. Julio Puyol (Madrid: Revista de Archivos, Bibliotecas y Museos, 1926) is a later medieval translation of the Latin text.

down to the fall of Seville in 1248 will assist the reader's understanding of the text.

Castile and León in the Twelfth and Thirteenth Centuries

After defeating the Visigothic King Rodrigo in the battle of the Guadalete in 711, Muslim invaders from Morocco overthrew the Visigoths who had established their rule in Spain (the *Hispania* of the Romans) about two hundred years before. Until the early eleventh century a Muslim unitary state centered at Córdoba dominated the peninsula, including the tiny Christian kingdoms that began to emerge in the northwest and in the foothills of the Pyrenees mountains. The apogee of Islamic Spain was reached when the emir of Córdoba determined in 929 to assume the title of caliph, thereby declaring himself to be the legitimate successor to the universal authority of the Prophet Muhammad. The glory of the caliphate lasted just a century, however, and came crashing to the ground in 1031. In place of one Muslim kingdom there now emerged nearly two dozen petty kingdoms, the so-called *taifas*, mutually jealous and often at war with one another. This situation provided a unique opportunity for the Christian rulers, who had been battered and bruised by Muslim armies over the centuries, to turn the tables and to demand tribute from the *taifas*.[3]

The largest and most important of the Christian states was the kingdom of León, whose antecedents derived from a band of warriors in Asturias who first challenged Muslim domination in the middle years of the eighth century. The kings of Asturias were able to advance the seat of their authority to the city of León by the beginning of the tenth century. Next in importance was Castile, originally a county subordinate to the kingdom of León, but lying ex-

---

[3] Joseph F. O'Callaghan, *A History of Medieval Spain* (Ithaca: Cornell University Press, 1975), 49–54, 91–136; Roger Collins, *The Arab Conquest of Spain, 710–797* (Oxford: Blackwell, 1994), and idem, *Early Medieval Spain. Unity in Diversity, 400–1000* (New York: St. Martin's Press, 1983), 146–224; W. Montgomery Watt, *A History of Islamic Spain* (Edinburgh: University Press, 1965), 5–80; Richard Fletcher, *Moorish Spain* (Berkeley: University of California Press, 1992), 1–105; Hugh Kennedy, *Muslim Spain and Portugal: A Political History of al-Andalus* (London and New York: Longman, 1996), 1–153; Derek W. Lomax, *The Reconquest of Spain* (London and New York: Longman, 1978), 10–48.

posed to Muslim attack on the eastern frontier. In the second half of the tenth
century, Fernán González, the count of Castile, effectively assured Castilian
autonomy within the kingdom of León. To the east of Castile running along
the Pyrenees were the tiny Basque kingdom of Navarre, centered at Pamplona; the county (and later kingdom) of Aragón; and several Catalan coun-
ties that were gradually brought under the rule of the count of Barcelona.[4]

In the early years of the eleventh century the king of Navarre, Sancho III
Garcés, better known as Sancho *el Mayor* or Sancho the Great (1000–1035),
succeeded in establishing his control over the neighboring county of Aragón;
he also married his oldest son into the Castilian comital house, and just before he died occupied the city of León itself. As a consequence, Sancho *el
Mayor* was able to provide each of his three sons with a kingdom: García III
(1035–1054) inherited the kingdom of Navarre; Ramiro I (1035–1063) received Aragón and assumed the title of king; and Fernando I (1035–1065),
along with the royal title, took control over Castile. Two years later he
seized the kingdom of León, thereby joining the two realms in a union that
would last until 1157.[5]

During the first three quarters of the eleventh century the Christians, especially Fernando I and his son Alfonso VI (1065–1109), king of León-Castile,
dominated the *taifas,* requiring them to pay annual tribute known as *parias.*
Simultaneously Fernando I pressed the reconquest by capturing Lamego and
Viseu in 1055 and Coimbra in 1064.[6] Continuing his father's policy of exact-
ing tribute from the petty Muslim rulers, Alfonso VI also achieved a conquest
of great symbolic importance when he occupied Toledo in 1085. Located on
the Tagus river, almost in the center of the Iberian peninsula, Toledo had
been the seat of the Visigothic kings. Now that it was in Alfonso VI's
possession he expressed his claims to hegemony over the entire peninsula,
including lands still under Muslim rule, by entitling himself "emperor of

---

[4] Collins, *Early Medieval Spain,* 225–268.

[5] O'Callaghan, *Medieval Spain,* 134–136; Justo Pérez de Urbel, *Sancho el Mayor de
Navarra* (Madrid: Consejo superior de Investigaciones científicas, 1950).

[6] David Wasserstein, *The Rise and Fall of the Party Kings, 1002–1086* (Princeton:
Princeton University Press, 1985); Bernard F. Reilly, *The Contest of Christian and Muslim Spain, 1031–1157* (Oxford: Blackwell, 1992), 1–49; Angus MacKay, *Spain in the
Middle Ages. From Frontier to Empire, 1000–1500* (New York: St. Martin's Press, 1983),
15–35.

Spain" (*imperator Hispanie*). That gesture proved to be premature, however, because the Muslim rulers, rather than await inevitable absorption into the Christian kingdoms, appealed to the sect of the Almoravids, who were busily establishing their control over Morocco. As a result, the Almoravids invaded Spain and inflicted a major defeat on Alfonso VI at Zalaca (Sagrajas) near Badajoz in 1086. In the next several years the Almoravids swallowed up the petty Muslim kingdoms and unified Islamic Spain once again; in the circumstances the Christians were no longer able to exact tribute from the Muslims.[7]

The possibility that the Christian states might achieve a comparable unity to counterbalance the Almoravids arose when Alfonso VI's daughter Urraca, queen of León-Castile (1109–1126), married Alfonso I, the Battler, king of Aragón and Navarre (1104–1134). Such a union was not to be, however, because of the incompatibility of the wedded pair.[8] After their separation Alfonso I directed his energy to the reconquest, and in 1118 succeeded in taking Zaragoza on the Ebro river. Though his dominions were greatly increased, he died before he was able to complete the conquest of other towns along the river.[9]

As the peoples of Aragón and Navarre opted to elect different kings, the union of the two kingdoms achieved in 1076 was dissolved.[10] In Aragón, Alfonso I's brother, Ramiro II (1134–1137), came out of a monastery to mount the throne and to father a child, Petronila. After arranging her betrothal to Count Ramon Berenguer IV of Barcelona in 1137, Ramiro withdrew to his monastery. The count, assuming the title of Prince of Aragón, took respon-

---

[7] Bernard F. Reilly, *The Kingdom of León-Castilla under King Alfonso VI, 1065–1109* (Princeton: Princeton University Press, 1988), and idem, *The Contest of Christian and Muslim Spain*, 74–125; Lomax, *The Reconquest of Spain*, 49–80; Watt, *A History of Islamic Spain*, 95–102; Fletcher, *Moorish Spain*, 106–111; Kennedy, *Muslim Spain and Portugal*, 130–153.

[8] Bernard F. Reilly, *The Kingdom of León-Castilla under Queen Urraca, 1109–1126* (Princeton: Princeton University Press, 1982); Lomax, *The Reconquest of Spain*, 80–85.

[9] Reilly, *The Contest of Christian and Muslim Spain*, 157–180; Thomas N. Bisson, *The Medieval Crown of Aragon. A Short History* (Oxford: Clarendon Press, 1986), 5–30; Fletcher, *Moorish Spain*, 111–115; Kennedy, *Muslim Spain and Portugal*, 154–188.

[10] When Sancho IV of Navarre was assassinated in 1076, his second cousin, Sancho I of Aragón, invaded Navarre, occupied Pamplona, and was recognized as king. Thus Aragón and Navarre were united under one ruler until 1134.

sibility for governing both that kingdom and his own county.[11] The union of Aragón and Barcelona, effected in this way, altered the political landscape in Spain, by creating a state with great potential for further expansion in the peninsula. At the same time, in the west, the county of Portugal, an extension of the kingdom of León, had also emerged as an autonomous entity under Alfonso VI's daughter Teresa and her French husband, Count Henry of Burgundy. Their son, Afonso I Henriques (1128–1185), proclaimed himself king of Portugal. Thus the union of the kingdom of Aragón and the county of Barcelona on the east and the *de facto* existence of the kingdom of Portugal on the west raised an effective challenge to the claims of the kings of León-Castile to dominance over all of Christian Spain.[12]

The task of trying to maintain ascendancy within the new political configuration of Christian Spain fell to Alfonso VII (1126–1157) of León-Castile, the son of Queen Urraca and her first husband, Count Raymond of Burgundy.[13] In the meantime, the Almoravid regime had begun to disintegrate both in Morocco and in Spain, with the result that a new group of petty Muslim kingdoms appeared in the peninsula. Now all of the Christian rulers endeavored to take advantage of this unstable situation. Thus Alfonso VII, with the collaboration of Count Ramon Berenguer IV and a Genoese fleet, captured the port of Almería on the southeastern coast in October 1147. A week later Afonso I of Portugal, helped by a northern European fleet participating in the Second Crusade, captured Lisbon at the mouth of the Tagus river. In the next two years Ramon Berenguer IV seized Tortosa and Lérida and completed the conquest of the Ebro river valley.[14]

---

[11] O'Callaghan, *Medieval Spain,* 193–214; Bisson, *The Medieval Crown of Aragon,* 16–17, 27–31.

[12] Reilly, *The Contest of Christian and Muslim Spain,* 141–156, 200–204; A. H. de Oliveira Marques, *History of Portugal,* 2d ed., 2 vols. (New York: Columbia University Press, 1976), 1:1–59; Harold V. Livermore, *A New History of Portugal* (Cambridge: Cambridge University Press, 1966), 1–53.

[13] Bernard F. Reilly, *The Kingdom of León-Castilla under King Alfonso VII, 1126–1157* (Philadelphia: University of Pennsylvania Press, 1998); Lomax, *The Reconquest of Spain,* 86–93.

[14] O'Callaghan, *Medieval Spain,* 215–233; Reilly, *The Contest of Christian and Muslim Spain,* 205–230; Livermore, *A New History of Portugal,* 54–60. See also *De expugnatione Lyxbonensi. The Conquest of Lisbon,* ed. and trans. Charles W. David (New York: Columbia University Press, 1936).

The possibility of continued Christian advance was checked, however, by the Almohads, another Muslim sect, who came to power in Morocco on the ruins of the Almoravid empire, and then invaded Spain. Once again the Christians were put on the defensive. Alfonso VII died in 1157 after failing to prevent the Almohads from taking Almería. The king unfortunately divided his kingdoms between two sons, giving Castile to the eldest, Sancho III (1157–1158), and León to Fernando II (1157–1188). The separation of the two kingdoms created a rivalry between them that was not resolved until their reunification in 1230. The second half of the twelfth century was filled with warfare between the Christians and the Almohads who not only imposed their authority over all of Islamic Spain, but also attempted to recover lands that had been taken by the Christians.[15]

The high point of this conflict came in 1195 when the Almohad caliph thoroughly defeated Alfonso VIII of Castile (1158–1214) and threatened Toledo itself. Eventually a series of truces prompted by the caliph's need to attend to Moroccan affairs gave the Christians a respite, but they used that to renew warfare among themselves. The papacy attempted to intervene and to recall the Christian rulers to their senses, reminding them that they ought to focus their energy on overcoming the Almohads. As the truce with the Almohads came to an end, Alfonso VIII appealed to his fellow Christian rulers to join him in a campaign against the enemy. The pope conferred crusading indulgences on all those who participated, and a substantial contingent of crusaders from southern France responded. The climax came when the Christian and Almohad armies met on the battlefield of Las Navas de Tolosa in 1212. This time, the victory went to the Christians.[16]

As a consequence, Alfonso VIII assured the security of Toledo and opened up the possibility of a Christian advance into the Guadalquivir valley in Andalucía. Moreover, the Almohad regime also began to decline and the

---

[15] O'Callaghan, *Medieval Spain*, 234–242; Livermore, *A New History of Portugal*, 61–66; Julio González, *Regesta de Fernando II* (Madrid: Consejo superior de Investigaciones científicas, 1943); Kennedy, *Muslim Spain and Portugal*, 189–236.

[16] O'Callaghan, *Medieval Spain*, 243–249; Lomax, *The Reconquest of Spain*, 112–128; Watt, *A History of Islamic Spain*, 103–110; Fletcher, *Moorish Spain*, 105–130; Kennedy, *Muslim Spain and Portugal*, 237–255; Julio González, *El reino de Castilla en la época de Alfonso VIII*, 3 vols. (Madrid: Consejo superior de Investigaciones científicas, 1960).

caliphs lost their grip on Spain, so much so that in the second quarter of the thirteenth century the unity of Islamic Spain was shattered, as individual Muslim lords clamored for power. That situation worked to the advantage of the Christians again and made possible the great conquests of the thirteenth century. In the east Jaime I of Aragón (1213–1276) conquered the island of Mallorca in 1229, the first stage in Catalan expansion into the Mediterranean. Then from 1232 to 1238 he steadily subjugated the Muslim kingdom of Valencia, pushing his frontier as far south as it would go. In effect, he created the Crown of Aragón with its constituents, the kingdoms of Aragón, Mallorca, and Valencia, and the county of Barcelona.[17] In the west, during the reigns of Sancho II (1223–1248) and Afonso III (1248–1279), the Portuguese steadily occupied the fortresses of the Alémtejo, the region south of Lisbon and the Tagus river, and the Algarve, the southernmost part of Portugal. By virtue of their efforts the kingdom of Portugal achieved the boundaries that it has retained, with some modification, until the present.[18]

In the meantime, in the center of the peninsula, Alfonso IX of León (1188–1230) and his son, Fernando III (1217–1252) of Castile, carried out a series of campaigns along the Muslim frontier. The capture of Cáceres, Mérida, and Badajoz climaxed the long reign of Alfonso IX; but on his death in 1230 his kingdom was claimed by his son, who thus brought about the reunion of León and Castile. With the resources of both kingdoms at his disposal Fernando III conquered Córdoba in 1236 and received the submission of the Muslim lords of Murcia, who acknowledged him as their suzerain in 1244, promising to pay an annual tribute. Then in 1246 he seized Jaén and two years later forced the surrender of Seville.[19] As a result the greater part of Spain was now under Christian rule. Only the kingdom of Granada remained

[17] O'Callaghan, *Medieval Spain*, 340–343, 345–349; Bisson, *The Medieval Crown of Aragon*, 58–85. A major source of these events is Jaime I's account of his military campaigns: *The Chronicle of James I, King of Aragon*, trans. J. Forster, 2 vols. (London: Chapman and Hall, 1883).

[18] O'Callaghan, *Medieval Spain*, 349–351; Livermore, *A New History of Portugal*, 67–80; Oliveira Marques, *History of Portugal*, 1:59–84.

[19] O'Callaghan, *Medieval Spain*, 333–357; Lomax, *The Reconquest of Spain*, 129–159; MacKay, *Spain in the Middle Ages*, 36–58; Julio González, *Alfonso IX*, 2 vols. (Madrid: Consejo superior de Investigaciones científicas, 1945), and idem, *Reinado y diplomas de Fernando III*, 3 vols. (Córdoba: Monte de Piedad y Caja de Ahorros, 1980–1986); Kennedy, *Muslim Spain and Portugal*, 256–279.

in Muslim hands, but the king of Granada recognized Fernando III as his
overlord and pledged to pay tribute each year. That situation would remain
in effect until the final conquest by Ferdinand and Isabella in 1492.[20]

The Latin Chronicle of the Kings of Castile

With that background in mind we can now consider the distinguishing
characteristics and specific virtues of the Latin Chronicle of the Kings of Castile.

The Manuscript and Editions
The Latin Chronicle has not been as widely known and used as some other
narrative sources, in part because of difficulties posed by the manuscript and
the first edition of the text. In 1912 Georges Cirot edited the Chronicle for
the first time, giving it the title Chronique latine des rois de Castille jusqu'en
1236.[21] Since then historians are in agreement in calling it the Crónica latina
de los reyes de Castilla or Latin Chronicle of the Kings of Castile. Luis Charlo
Brea, in his most recent edition, entitled it Chronica latina regum Castellae.[22]

Thus far, the text of the Chronicle has been found in only one manuscript:
Madrid, Biblioteca de la Real Academia de la Historia, 9/450 (formerly G–1),

---

[20] Lomax, *The Reconquest of Spain*, 160–178; Watt, *A History of Islamic Spain*, 147–
165; Fletcher, *Moorish Spain*, 157–177; Kennedy, *Muslim Spain and Portugal*, 280–304;
L. P. Harvey, *Islamic Spain, 1250 to 1500* (Chicago: University of Chicago Press,
1990).

[21] Georges Cirot, "Une chronique latine inédite des rois de Castille jusqu'en
1236," *Bulletin Hispanique* 14 (1912): 30–46, 109–118, 244–274, 353–374; 15 (1913):
18–37, 170–187, 268–283, 411–427. I use the offprint: *Chronique latine des rois de
Castille jusqu'en 1236* (Bordeaux: Feret et Fils, 1913). He revised his edition in 1920:
"Une chronique latine inédite des rois de Castille (1236)," *Bulletin Hispanique* 22
(1920): 1–153. See also Cirot's studies of the text: "Appendices à la Chronique latine
des Rois de Castille," *Bulletin Hispanique* 17 (1915): 101–115, 243–258; 20 (1918):
27–35, 149–184; 21 (1919): 173–192; also idem, "Recherches sur la Chronique latine
des Rois de Castille," *Bulletin Hispanique* 21 (1919): 193–217, 276–281; 25 (1923):
97–107.

[22] *Chronica latina regum Castellae*, in *Chronica Hispana Saeculi XIII*, ed. Luis Charlo
Brea, Juan A. Estévez Sola, and Rocío Carande Herrero, Corpus Christianorum Continuatio Mediaevalis 73 (Turnhout: Brepols, 1997), 9–118; see 23–29 for a discussion
of the manuscript transmission and a critique of the editions of Cirot and Cabanes
Pecourt.

folios 89–122. The codex containing the text of the *Chronicle* dates from the end of the fifteenth century and bears the title on the cover *Chronica b. Isidori iun. et aliorum;* it consists of 280 parchment folios and was written in a Gothic script probably by Lorenzo Galíndez de Carvajal (historian and councillor to Ferdinand and Isabella) or someone acting at his direction. In the late eighteenth century the Aragonese scholar Manuel Abella cited the importance of the *Latin Chronicle,* and made a transcript of the text contained in the codex mentioned above, but his plans for publication fell through. His transcription is now located in the British Library, Egerton 1125; it should be emphasized that it is a copy of the only known manuscript of the *Latin Chronicle* and not an original version.[23]

Cirot's edition was a palaeographical one and thus not always easy to use. His copious annotations, however, are quite valuable. Pointing to the difficulty that one might encounter in reading Cirot's text and the scarcity of copies in Spain at that time, María Desamparados Cabanes Pecourt produced another edition in 1964, entitling it *Crónica latina de los reyes de Castilla.* Her introduction to the *Chronicle* was comparatively brief and her transcriptions sometimes made no sense; she also did not attempt to annotate the text, other than to explain some of her readings. Although she published a second and a third edition correcting some earlier deficiencies,[24] her work has been superseded by that of Luis Charlo Brea. In 1984 he edited the *Chronicle* with the title *Crónica latina de los reyes de Castilla,* along with a Spanish translation on facing pages and a critique of the work of his predecessors.[25] Thirteen years later he edited the text once again as the *Chronica latina regum Castellae.*[26] That edition is now to be preferred to all others. His principal concern was to establish an accurate transcription of the text, making it readable and intelligible, and to record variations between his readings and those of his

---

[23] As the royal chancellor, Bishop Juan of Osma, is believed to have been the author of the Chronicle (see below), it is likely that the original manuscript was written in the chancery hand. For an example of that see the facsimile of the treaty of Tordehumos of 1194 in González, *Alfonso VIII,* 1:712, facing page.

[24] María Desamparados Cabanes Pecourt, *Crónica latina de los reyes de Castilla* (Valencia: Anubar, 1964, 1985). Charlo Brea commented (27–28) that this was not a critical edition, and that her punctuation sometimes obscured the meaning of the text.

[25] Luis Charlo Brea, *Crónica latina de la reyes de Castilla* (Cádiz: Universidad de Cádiz, 1984).

[26] Charlo Brea, *Chronica latina* (above n. 22)

predecessors. His numerous references to biblical citations in the text are most helpful. Although he provided a few explanatory notes to the text, he did not attempt to explicate in any detail the events being described. Recently he also issued separately a revised Spanish translation of the *Chronicle,* which does include many explanatory notes.[27]

The text of the *Chronicle* lacks a title and there are scarcely any internal divisions; the initials of each paragraph are missing, probably with the intention that they would be supplied later by an illuminator. There are numerous abbreviations. If there ever had been an introductory section to the *Chronicle* explaining the author's intent — and I suspect there was — it is now missing. Cirot divided it into three sections; but if one counts his two subdivisions in section two and the four in section three, then there are seven sections all told. He also divided the text into seventy-five chapters of varying length. Neither Cabanes Pecourt nor Charlo Brea initially preserved Cirot's divisions, though both divided the text into unnumbered paragraphs and endeavored to resolve the abbreviations that Cirot had allowed to stand. In his latest edition Charlo Brea adopted Cirot's division into seventy-five numbered paragraphs, while criticizing it as sometimes arbitrary.

The Date of Composition

The text of the *Chronicle,* though found in a fifteenth-century manuscript, originated some two hundred years before. The work is undated, but internal clues reveal that the author wrote it during the reigns of Alfonso VIII and Fernando III. Derek Lomax, Cabanes Pecourt, and Charlo Brea have all attempted to establish the date or dates of composition. According to Lomax, the author began to write the *Chronicle* after Afonso II ascended the Portuguese throne in 1211 (chaps. 2, 18),[28] and prior to the death of Louis VIII of

---

[27] *Crónica latina de los reyes de Castilla,* trans. Luis Charlo Brea (Madrid: Akal, 1999). In my copy pages 98–99 (chaps. 69–71), 102–103 (chaps. 73–76), 106–108, 110–111, 114–115, 118–119, 122–123 unfortunately were left blank.

[28] In chap. 2 the author provides a genealogy of the first kings of Portugal, namely Afonso I (1126–1185), Sancho I (1185–1211), and Afonso II (1211–1223): "scilicet regem Aldefonsum Portugalie, qui fuit pater regis Sancii, patris regis Alfonsi." In chap. 18 he records the marriage of Alfonso VIII's daughter Urraca to Afonso (the future Afonso II), the son of King Sancho I of Portugal: "tradidit in uxorem Alfonso, filio Sancii, regis Portugalie, qui postea regnauit pro patre suo Sancio." The marriage took place in 1208.

France (1223–1226). The latter was described as the king "who now reigns" — "qui nunc regnat" — and his wife Blanca of Castile as the one "who is now the crowned queen of the French" — "qui nunc est coronata regina Francorum" (chap. 18). The reference to Alfonso IX of León as the king "who now reigns in place of his father" — "qui nunc pro patre regnat" (chap. 11) — indicates that the author was at work on the *Chronicle* prior to the Leonese king's death on 24 September 1230. The author's remark concerning the accession of Fernando III — "truly indeed was this a useful pretext for the Castilians, for if it had not been done so prudently, perhaps today they would not have their own king" (chap. 33) — makes plain that this section of the *Chronicle* was written before Fernando III succeeded to the Leonese throne in 1230.[29]

Cabanes Pecourt and Charlo Brea believe that the *Chronicle* was written in two stages, the first extending to the capture of Capilla in 1226, and the second to the fall of Córdoba in 1236. Cabanes suggested that the statement that "the *Mahdî*, who was called 'Abd al-Mu'min, ... deprived the Almoravid lords of their kingdom ... [and] when he had accomplished these things, ... his descendants were deprived of their kingdom in our day (privatus est regno in posteris suis in diebus nostris)" (chap. 45)[30] refers to the assassination of the Almohad Caliph 'Abd al-Wâhid, which can be dated on 7 September 1224. On that basis one may conclude that the first section of the *Chronicle* was written between September 1224 and November 1226, when Louis VIII died. Given the fact that the Spanish era was employed to date events up to the conquest of Capilla in August 1226 and that events thereafter were usually recorded according to the year of the Lord, Cabanes and Charlo Brea agree that the first section was likely completed between August and November 1226. The second section of the *Chronicle* was probably written after November 1236, when the king returned to Burgos after the settlement of the newly reconquered city of Córdoba (chap. 75), and before May

[29] Derek W. Lomax, "The Authorship of the *Chronique latine des rois de Castille*," *Bulletin of Hispanic Studies* 40 (1963): 205–211, here 205.

[30] Cabanes originally in 1964 read this passage as "privatus est regno in potestis suis in diebus nostris," following the manuscript, whereas Charlo Brea read *in posteris* in place of *in potestis*, following conjectures by Cirot and Cabanes Pecourt in 1985. The conjectured reading makes more sense.

1239, when Álvar Pérez de Castro sold Paredes de Nava to the Order of Calatrava (chap. 65).[31]

My own sense is that the author labored on the *Chronicle* on a more or less continuing basis. The manner in which he reports events year by year from the latter part of the reign of Alfonso VIII down to the conquest of Córdoba suggests that he regularly added to the *Chronicle*. So I see it as an ongoing enterprise, probably begun late in the reign of Alfonso VIII.

The Author

The *Latin Chronicle* is an anonymous work in that no author's name is associated with it. Cirot raised the possibility that the chronicler might be either Bishop Domingo of Plasencia or Bishop Juan of Osma, but ultimately he concluded that there was no way of determining authorship.[32] Cabanes Pecourt expressed the opinion in her first edition of 1964 that the author was Archbishop Rodrigo Jiménez de Rada, but his style is totally different from that of the *Latin Chronicle,* and there seems no reason why he would have written an account covering much the same ground as his *History of the Affairs of Spain.* Cabanes Pecourt has since abandoned that suggestion.[33]

Some years ago Derek Lomax argued that the author was Juan, the royal chancellor of Castile from 1217 until his death in 1246.[34] About twenty years prior to Lomax's article, Luciano Serrano, without reference to the *Latin Chronicle,* provided the details of Juan's biography, insofar as they were known. Building on biographical data provided by Serrano, Lomax studied the *Latin Chronicle* in detail looking for clues as to the identity of the author. On the basis of those clues, which are summarized below, he concluded that the author was the chancellor, Juan, bishop of Osma and later of Burgos. Both Cabanes Pecourt and Charlo Brea, as well as historians generally,[35] have accepted Lomax's identification of the chancellor, Bishop Juan of Osma, as

---

[31] Cabanes Pecourt, *Crónica latina,* 10; Charlo Brea, *Chronica latina,* 18–19.

[32] Georges Cirot, "Recherches sur la Chronique latine des Rois de Castille," *Bulletin Hispanique* 21 (1919): 193–217.

[33] Cabanes Pecourt, *Crónica latina,* 10–12.

[34] Lomax, "Authorship," (above n. 28). Charlo Brea, *Chronica latina,* 11–18, without rejecting Lomax's essential position, summarized all the arguments concerning authorship.

[35] See for example Peter Linehan, *History and the Historians of Medieval Spain* (Oxford: Clarendon Press, 1993), 320, 325 n., 526.

the author of the *Chronicle*. Among them, Julio González provided additional information concerning his life.[36]

Juan the chancellor probably came from the area around Soria in the diocese of Osma in Old Castile, but efforts to determine his family of origin are inconclusive. Some suggested that his *apellido* or family name was Domínguez, but that appears to be based on a faulty reading of texts.[37] The *Chronicle* offers numerous indications that the author was a native of Old Castile who was thoroughly familiar with the landscape, even to the point of naming small villages (chaps. 31–39). Lomax commented that he was very much interested in the "political faction fights" north of the Duero river, and that he was concerned with the region south of the Duero only insofar as it involved the reconquest. As a consequence, the author has much to say about the activities of the Lara family, who dominated much of that area of Castile. Perhaps on that same account, the author's comments on Diego López de Haro, lord of Vizcaya, head of another prominent family in the region, are quite positive, even when we know from other sources that his behavior and that of other members of his family were not always exemplary (chaps. 13, 17, 24, 28, 65).

Like many other Castilian ecclesiastics in the late twelfth century, Juan the chancellor probably studied at one of the emerging universities, such as Bologna or Paris, receiving training in the seven liberal arts, in philosophy, theology, and canon law.[38] Quite possibly he studied in Paris, as did his prede-

---

[36] Luciano Serrano, "El canciller de Fernando III de Castilla," *Hispania* (1941): 3–40; González, *Fernando III*, 1:504–509, and idem, "La Crónica latina de los reyes de Castilla," *Homenaje a don Agustín Millares Carlo*, 2 vols. (Palma: Caja Insular de Ahorros de Gran Canaria, 1975), 2:55–70.

[37] Agustín Millares Carlo, "La cancillería real en León y Castilla hasta fines del reinado de Fernando III," *Anuario de Historia del Derecho Español* 3 (1926): 282–283. González, *Fernando III*, 1:505, cited a document of 1235 in which Miguel González, brother of the chancellor — "ermano del chanceler" — granted property to the monastery of San Pedro de Gumiel. One would expect that Juan would also adopt his father's name, Gonzalo, and be known as Juan González; Serrano commented that it was not the custom for ecclesiastics to be identified by patronymic in that way. See also Pedro Fernández Martín, "El Obispo de Osma, canciller de Fernando III el Santo, no se llamaba don Juan Domínguez," *Celtiberia* 27 (1964): 79–95.

[38] Lomax, "Authorship," 206, suggested that he may have been one of the many *magistri* who were returning at this period to important positions in the Spanish church after studying in a foreign university such as Bologna or Paris.

cessor as chancellor, Diego García.[39] The author of the *Chronicle* was evidently a well-educated ecclesiastic who usually dated events according to religious festivals and easily cited the classical authors Lucan (chap. 2), Virgil (chap. 14), Horace (chap. 18), and Claudian (chap. 23). Charlo Brea called attention to his many biblical references; he frequently quoted passages from Genesis, the Psalms, Maccabees, Daniel, Judges, Jonah, and Sirach. Less common are his citations of the New Testament: Mark, Luke, Romans, and Revelation.[40] His frequent (six) references to the problem of consanguinity in royal marriages (chaps. 10, 11, 14, 15, 32, 65) suggest that his training was in canon law. Indeed in one instance (chap. 2), which neither Cirot nor Charlo Brea nor Cabanes Pecourt was able to resolve, and to which Lomax did not allude, he provides an exact citation from Gratian's *Decretum*. That alone would suggest a more than passing knowledge of canon law. His reference (chap. 35) to bringing "agreement out of the discord of disagreement" — "discordiam discordantium ad concordiam reuocauit" — sounds like a play on the formal title of Gratian's work, *Concordia discordantium canonum*. Whether he was a master of canon law or a master of arts is not known, but one or the other seems quite likely.

González suggested that Juan may have accompanied Bishop Diego of Osma and St. Dominic, then a canon of Osma, on their journey in 1205 to southern France, where they observed the widespread character of the Albigensian heresy. From there they continued on to Rome where they expressed their concern about the extent of the heresy to Pope Innocent III.[41] The author of the *Chronicle* tells us (chap. 30) that he witnessed the papal consecration of the first Latin Patriarch of Constantinople in Rome in March 1205. That might explain the particular attention given by the *Chronicle* to the Albigensian heresy and to the Latin Empire of Constantinople. González suggested that references to the affairs of the Latin Empire may have been prompted by Fernando III's queen, Beatriz of Swabia, a granddaughter of the

---

[39] Diego García, *Planeta,* ed. Manuel Alonso (Madrid: Consejo superior de Investigaciones científicas, 1943), 42, 125–130. Alonso suggested that Juan Díaz, whom he identified as the later chancellor, was a son of Diego García, but there is no proof of that.

[40] Biblical citations can be tracked in Charlo Brea's 1997 index, 213–218 under the siglum "C", and other quotations, 219–224, also under "C".

[41] González, *Alfonso VIII,* 1: 427–429.

Byzantine Emperor Isaac Angelus and a niece of Emperor Alexius Angelus. Perhaps Juan also enjoyed a close association with Diego's successor as bishop of Osma, Rodrigo Jiménez de Rada; when the latter was elected archbishop of Toledo in 1209, Juan may have accompanied him and found a place in the royal court.

In any case, he probably first found employment in the court of Alfonso VIII as a scribe, and may perhaps be identified with the Juan who appears as subnotary there from 1209 to 1212. González was skeptical of the suggestion that he might be identified with Juan Díaz, a notary, whose name appears in documents of 1215–1217.[42] The author also tells us that he attended the Fourth Lateran Council in Rome in 1215 (chap. 30), perhaps in the entourage of Archbishop Rodrigo, or of the then chancellor Diego García.[43] His easy familiarity with the royal family is reflected in his frequent references to the illnesses of Alfonso VIII and Queen Leonor (chaps. 20, 26, 28) and his identification of the royal physician, Master Arnaldo (chap. 21).

Queen Berenguela, whom he named as one of the executors of his will, certainly was responsible for his appointment as chancellor of Castile upon the accession of her son Fernando III in 1217.[44] Now by royal privilege the office of chancellor was held by the archbishop of Toledo, but that was essentially an honorific position. The actual work of the chancery, supervising notaries and scribes, and drafting, issuing, and registering all royal privileges and charters was Juan's responsibility. In order to act as chancellor he had to have the consent of Archbishop Rodrigo Jiménez de Rada.

Several passages in the *Chronicle* imply that the author was familiar with the workings of the royal chancery and was able to consult royal archival materials when he wished to do so. He refers, for example, to "a certain charter, confirmed by his [Alfonso VIII's] leaden seal, which was issued in the curia celebrated at Carrión, and which was found in the armarium of the cathedral of Burgos" (chap. 33). He knew too the terms of the agreement between Fernando III and his sisters, settling the succession to the throne of

---

[42] González, *Fernando III*, 1:504.

[43] Diego García is listed in the *Acta* of the Council as one of the participants: see Juan Francisco Rivera Recio, "Personajes hispanos asistentes en 1215 al IV Concilio de Letrán. Revisión y aportación nueva de documentos. Datos biográficos," *Hispania Sacra* 4 (1951): 335–355.

[44] His first appearance as chancellor was in September 1217.

León in 1230 (chap. 61), and the pact concluded by Fernando III and Ibn Hûd, the Muslim king of Murcia (chap. 67), and he read the letters of Jaime I of Aragón recounting the conquest of Mallorca (chap. 55). When describing treaties or other agreements he used the language of the chancery; for example, "the form of the agreement was this" — "Forma uero compositionis hec erat" (chap. 61), or "the pact was confirmed under the aforesaid condition and a truce was also granted and confirmed" — "firmatum est pactum sub predicta conditione data insuper treuga et firmata" (chap. 73; cf. chap. 66). His references to the sums of money demanded in tribute by Fernando III from the petty Muslim kings also betoken a royal official who was in a position to know (chaps. 67, 73). On two occasions he mentions the bishop of Osma but clarifies the reference by adding that he was also the chancellor (chaps. 65, 73).

Juan's description of the circumstances surrounding Berenguela's renunciation of the throne in favor of her son at Valladolid in 1217 seems to be the work of someone who witnessed the entire series of events (chaps. 32, 34–35). In that very same year Juan also appeared as abbot of Santander. As the author of the *Chronicle,* he spoke harshly about the people of Gascony (chap. 17), probably reflecting the attitude of the people of Santander, who often engaged Gascon seamen in naval combat in the Bay of Biscay. After serving as abbot of Santander for two years, he became abbot of the Collegiate Church of Valladolid in 1219. In that capacity he took part in the Council of Valladolid held by the papal legate, Cardinal Jean d'Abbeville, in 1228, and joined him on his visitation of various sees in 1228 and 1229 and at the Council of Tarazona in Aragón. From the legate he learned of the planned conversion of the Muslim king of Valencia (chap. 54).

After Fernando III became king of León in 1230, he asked Archbishop Pedro of Compostela, who was the titular chancellor of the kingdom of León, to allow Juan to act as chancellor of León; in that way he united the chancery functions of both kingdoms in his own person (13 September 1231).[45] His faithful service to the crown was rewarded when he was elected bishop of Osma in April 1231. As such he initiated construction of the

---

[45] For Juan's letters acknowledging that he held the chancellorship of Castile from Archbishop Rodrigo (1 January 1230) and that of León from Archbishop Bernardo (13 September 1231), see Millares Carlo, "La cancillería real en León y Castilla," 286–288.

cathedral there.[46] We know from the *Chronicle* (chaps. 73–74) that after the surrender of Córdoba in 1236 Bishop Juan cleansed the mosque which was transformed into a cathedral, and then celebrated the first mass there and preached a sermon commemorating the triumph of Christian arms.

Although Juan was elected bishop of León in 1237, Fernando III appealed to Pope Gregory IX, arguing that he needed to retain the services of a faithful minister of the crown. The pope agreed and ordered the canons to elect someone else (2 December 1237).[47] Three years later, however, the king raised no objection to Juan's election as bishop of Burgos. When he was named bishop of Burgos,[48] he formally acknowledged that he held the office of chancellor with the consent of Archbishop Rodrigo (8 June 1240).[49]

Fernando III's confidence in his chancellor was such that he entrusted him with the education of his fifth son, Infante Felipe. Intended for an ecclesiastical career, Felipe was named a prebendary of the cathedral of Burgos when he was fifteen. The bishop also arranged to send him to study at the University of Paris, perhaps because Juan himself had studied there in his youth. Although Juan was not primarily a scholar, he enjoyed the esteem of his contemporaries. Bishop Lucas of Tuy described him as "sapientissimus," "most learned." The distinguished scholar, Hermann the German, evidently admired him and translated Aristotle's *Rhetoric* and *Poetics* from Arabic to Latin at the request of "the venerable father Bishop Juan of Burgos, chancellor of the king of Castile."[50]

---

[46] Charlo Brea, *Chronica latina*, 16–17, suggested that two nearly contemporaneous references may be taken as confirmation of Juan's authorship. The first time he confirmed a royal charter as chancellor and bishop of Osma was 17 October 1232. He was also identified for the first time in the *Chronicle* as bishop of Osma and chancellor in chap. 65 dealing with the excommunication of Lope Díaz and Álvar Pérez at Eastertime 1233.

[47] Lucien Auvray, *Les registres de Grégoire IX*, 2 vols. (Paris: Bibliothèque des Ecoles françaises d'Athènes et de Rome, 1896–1955), nos. 3967–3968.

[48] See Auvray, *Grégoire IX*, nos. 5075 (6 March 1239), 5189 (29 May 1240).

[49] Millares Carlo, "La cancillería real en León y Castilla," 288. This was done because the bishopric of Burgos was not part of the archdiocese of Toledo, as the bishopric of Osma was.

[50] Antonio Ballesteros, *Alfonso X, el Sabio* (Barcelona, 1963; repr. Barcelona: El Albir, 1984), 251–252: "Opus presentis translationis Rhetoricae Aristotelis et ejus Poeticae, ex arabico eloquio in latinam jamdudum intuitu venerabilis patris Johannis Burgensis episcopi et regis Castellae cancellarii."

As bishop of Burgos Juan died at Palencia on 1 October 1246. Three days before (28 September) he drew up his will,[51] naming as his executors Queen Berenguela, Archbishop Rodrigo of Toledo, Master Mateo, the dean of Burgos, Gonzalo Pérez, archdeacon of Valpuesta, and Pedro Martínez, the royal notary. He was buried in the cathedral of Burgos in the chapel of the Nativity of the Virgin Mary.[52]

Quite possibly Juan undertook the task of writing the *Chronicle* at the behest of Alfonso VIII or of the titular royal chancellor, Martín de Pisuerga, Archbishop of Toledo, for whom he had words of high praise (chap. 12). As the *Chronicle* reveals, Juan's relations with the royal family were close and intimate. He consistently described Alfonso VIII as "our glorious king" and Fernando III as "our lord the king," and spoke in admiring terms of Queen Berenguela. It is obvious that he had a direct contemporary knowledge of events, that he is at times an eyewitness or in a position to secure accurate information from others. Moreover, he had an exceptional familiarity with the general European scene, as Lomax pointed out: "In short the chronicler devotes to foreign affairs proportionately more space than any other Spanish historian of his age, and his comments are generally sensible, if unimaginative, the only curious one being his low opinion of the Gascons" (chap. 17).[53]

His chronology and his sense of geography are both quite exact. Lomax noted that especially from the end of the reign of Alfonso VIII, "he gives fairly precise dates for most of the events he relates" and that between 1214–1236 he provides "fifty-one dates that are all apparently accurate with the minor exception of that of Innocent III's death which is ascribed to the 15th instead of the 16th of July of 1216."[54] While he dates events on saints' days or other Christian festivals, he generally utilizes the chronological system in use in Spain for many centuries, the so-called era of Caesar, which is thirty-eight years in advance of the Christian era; thus era 1250 means A.D. 1212. At other times, especially when speaking about extrapeninsular affairs (chaps. 52, 54, 55, 58, 59) he uses the year of the Incarnation, or the year of grace

---

[51] For the will see Serrano, "El canciller de Fernando III de Castilla," 37–40, no. 4.

[52] Queen Berenguela died a month later on 8 November 1246; Pedro Martínez succeeded Juan as chancellor but he died in 1249.

[53] Lomax, "Authorship," 206–207.

[54] Lomax, "Authorship," 207–208.

(chaps. 65, 67), corresponding to our *anno Domini*. For the last dates given in the text, however, he reverts to the era of Caesar (chaps. 68, 69).

The language of the *Chronicle* is good ecclesiastical Latin, written in a straightforward manner with little rhetorical embellishment; the author eschewed hyperbole and fantasy. While he was obviously a churchman, a Christian, and a Castilian, with negative views of Saracens and other enemies of Castile, his narrative is clear and direct and likely truthful for the most part. There seems every reason to be believe that he should be identified with Juan the chancellor, bishop of Osma and later of Burgos.

Charlo Brea did raise on linguistic grounds the question whether another person may have written the final chapters (69 to 75) of the *Chronicle,* relating to the conquest of Córdoba. Nevertheless, he was unable to identify anyone as such and concluded that it was also possible that someone had reworked materials created by Bishop Juan.[55] Chapter 69 begins with the date "in the era written instead of that of Christ, namely, 1274 [A.D. 1236];" that suggests that the author was aware of the usage of the year of the Incarnation in several preceding chapters. Inasmuch as the bishop of Osma is twice referred to in the third person as the royal chancellor in chapters 70 and 73, it is possible that someone else wrote this section. Perhaps a cleric working for the bishop had that responsibility. One candidate might be Master Lope who "had first placed the standard of the cross on the tower" of the mosque of Córdoba, and then entered the mosque with the bishop of Osma to cleanse it and prepare its transformation into a Christian church (chap. 73). Master Lope may possibly be identified with the first bishop of Córdoba, elected in 1238 and consecrated in 1239.[56]

The Content of the Chronicle

The first section of the *Chronicle* (chaps. 1–8) extends from the death of Fernán González, count of Castile, in 970, to that of Sancho III, king of Castile, in 1158. After plunging the reader immediately into the late tenth century, the author traces the transformation of Castile from a county subor-

---

[55] Luis Charlo Brea, "¿Un segundo autor para la última parte de la *Crónica latina de los Reyes de Castilla?" Actas del I Congreso Nacional de Latín Medieval (León, 1–4 diciembre de 1993)* (León: Universidad de León, 1995): 251–256.

[56] González, *Fernando III,* 1:206.

dinate to the kingdom of León to an independent kingdom under the rule of Fernando I; the bare-bones genealogy given here is not entirely accurate (see the notes). The narrative then proceeds rapidly through the reign of Alfonso VI, who, after a struggle with his brothers, unified the inheritance of Castile and León. His conquest of Toledo in 1085 is cited, but the great invasion of the Almoravids of Morocco and their defeat of the king at Zalaca in 1086 is entirely neglected. Nor is there any mention of Rodrigo Díaz de Vivar, the Cid, who played such a prominent role in Castilian affairs in the late eleventh century. The problem of the succession to the throne receives some attention, and the marriages of Alfonso VI's daughters Urraca and Teresa to Raymond and Henry of Burgundy respectively are noted.

The turbulent reign of Urraca, who succeeded her father, is given short shrift, and it is obvious that the author holds her in disdain. On the contrary, he praises the warlike career of her second husband, Alfonso I of Aragón. Although he describes the king's siege of Fraga and his death, he says nothing about his conquest of Zaragoza in 1118. The succession question and the resulting union of Aragón and Catalonia are mentioned in a few words.

The triumphs of Urraca's son Alfonso VII over the Saracens and his capture of Almería are recorded, as well as the fact of his proclamation as emperor of León. What is particularly interesting in this section is the author's description of the rise of the Almohads, a new Muslim sect in Morocco, who played a major role in peninsular affairs in the second half of the twelfth century and the first quarter of the thirteenth. Before noting the death of Alfonso VII on his return journey from Muslim Spain, the author bemoans the troubles that arose from the king's division of León and Castile between his two sons Fernando II and Sancho III. This closes the first section.

In many respects the first section forms a sort of preamble to the second and third sections which constitute the bulk of the *Chronicle,* and summarizes the history of Castile from the late tenth century to the middle of the twelfth century, perhaps as it was known to the oral tradition of the royal court. In the latter two sections, which narrate the reigns of Alfonso VIII and Fernando III, the author is a contemporary and well-placed witness of the actions he describes.

The second section (chaps. 9–30) records the major events of the reign of Alfonso VIII from the middle of the twelfth to the beginning of the thirteenth century. After treating the disorders of the king's minority, the author takes up the king's marriage, comments briefly on his capture of Cuenca and his quarrels with his uncles Fernando II of León and Sancho VI of Navarre, and adds some reference to Portuguese affairs. Nevertheless, it seems apparent that the author's direct knowledge of the king's early years was limited.

His text becomes more extensive as his role as a contemporary witness increases. Thus, for example, he reports the antagonism that developed between Alfonso VIII and his young cousin, Alfonso IX of León, and dogged their relationship for many years thereafter. The great battle of Alarcos, when Alfonso VIII suffered a humiliating defeat at the hands of the Almohads in 1195, is recounted in great detail, and it seems likely that the author either participated in it or — which seems more likely — heard about from those who did. The hostility between the kings of Castile and León flared up again in the years immediately following the battle, but Alfonso VIII found a valuable ally in the young king of Aragón, Pedro II. Renewed conflict between Castile and Navarre also took place. Once peace was established among the Christian rulers of the peninsula, Alfonso VIII set out to secure the duchy of Gascony which he claimed as his wife's dowry. The author regards that as a misguided effort and emphasizes the joy in Castile when the king abandoned it.

As the truce with the Almohads came to an end, the king's oldest son and heir, Infante Fernando, prepared to take the field against the enemy but died suddenly causing great sorrow. The author's description of the young prince's appearance and noble qualities indicates that he knew him very well. The subsequent fall of Salvatierra to the Almohads, the diplomatic effort to enlist the support of Christian Europe in a crusade, the decisive Christian victory in the battle of Las Navas de Tolosa in 1212, and its aftermath are given ample treatment. The death of Alfonso VIII and that of his queen shortly afterward evoked a moving lamentation from the author, who obviously held them both in great esteem.

The author also displayed for the first time his interest in extrapeninsular affairs. After noting the expansion of the Albigensian heresy in southern France, he reports the death of Pedro II of Aragón while fighting against the crusaders led by Simon de Montfort. In addition, after describing the participation in the Third Crusade of the Holy Roman Emperor Frederick Barbarossa, Richard the Lionheart, king of England, and Philip Augustus, king of France, the author summarizes the Fourth Crusade which resulted in the conquest of Constantinople. He concludes this section by mentioning the Fourth Lateran Council of 1215 (which he attended), which proposed sweeping reforms for the church and also launched the Fifth Crusade, directed by the papal legate, Cardinal Pelagius, himself a Spaniard.

The third section (chaps. 31–75), concentrating on the reign of Fernando III down to the fall of Córdoba in 1236, also reflects the author's direct knowledge of circumstances and events. As preamble, he provides a brief narration of the reign of Alfonso VIII's son, Enrique I, and the struggle for power between his older sister Berenguela and Count Álvaro Núñez de Lara. The author's attention to detail and his adherence to Berenguela reveal him as an obviously interested, and indeed a partisan, witness. Enrique's accidental death raised the problem of the succession, which the author discusses at some length, telling us that Berenguela, who by right was entitled to the throne, insisted that the Castilians acknowledge as king her son, Fernando III, then seventeen. Although they did so, the young king's father, Alfonso IX, supported by Count Álvaro, endeavored to unite Castile to his own kingdom of León. Once the struggle for control of Castile was resolved in Fernando III's favor, the author tells us about his marriage to a granddaughter of Frederick Barbarossa and the suppression of various rebellious nobles. Attention is focused on John of Brienne, the king of Jerusalem, who married Fernando III's sister and subsequently became the titular Emperor of Constantinople.

Before Fernando III initiated his first campaign against the Moors, the author introduces a speech that the king supposedly made asking his mother's approbation. One need not take the text of the speech as a verbatim record, but it probably represents the gist of what the king had to say as reported by someone who heard him. There is a good narration of the civil conflict among the Almohads of Morocco and Spain which encouraged the king to take advantage of the situation. His campaigns in Andalucía and his relations with the petty Muslim kings of Baeza and Valencia, and the capture of Capilla in 1226, are related fully, as are the simultaneous military operations of the kings of León and Portugal against the Muslims.

An interlude follows as the author reports the wars of King Louis VIII of France against the Albigensian heretics and the eventual submission of Count Raymond VII of Toulouse to King Louis IX. This was of more than passing interest to the author and his readers because Louis VIII was married to Blanche of Castile, a daughter of Alfonso VIII and the mother of Louis IX.

Turning once again from France to Spain, the author describes the emergence of the Muslim leader Ibn Hûd, who represented the strongest challenge to Almohad rule in the peninsula. The mission to Spain of the papal legate, Cardinal Jean d'Abbeville, with whom the author had personal contact, is discussed. After a brief description of the conquest of Mallorca by Jaime I of Aragón and the campaigns of the kings of León and Portugal, extrapeninsular affairs, namely the Crusade of Emperor Frederick II and the subsequent conflict between papal and imperial forces in southern Italy, engage the reader.

Next, the author reports the death of Alfonso IX of León and Fernando III's succession to his father's throne, whereby Castile and León were now reunited. Though he still had to contend with hostile nobles, the king, as a consequence of the union, was now able to direct his energies entirely to the war against Islam. Interspersed here is a relation about the struggle of the pope and the Roman commune and the emperor's confrontation with the Lombard League. After the surprise entrance of some Christian troops into the city of Córdoba, the author devotes the remainder of the *Chronicle* to the conquest of that great Andalusian city in June 1236. Following his description of the king's triumphal reception in the city and his arrangements for its defense, the author concludes his work in November as the king made his way northward to Burgos. One may suspect that the author intended to continue the *Chronicle* as long as he was able to do so, but he broke off from his appointed task for reasons that are unknown to us.

This Translation

As the basis of this translation I have used Charlo Brea's edition of the *Chronica latina regum Castellae*, comparing it principally with that of Cirot, and secondarily with that of Cabanes Pecourt. I have divided the text into three sections: I. From Count Fernán González to King Sancho III (923–1158); II. The Reign of Alfonso VIII, King of Castile (1158–1214); III. The Reign of Fernando III, King of Castile-León, 1217–1252. I have also retained Cirot's chapter divisions because they facilitate easy reference. The titles of the three sections as well as the chapter headings are mine. One should also keep in mind that the title, *The Latin Chronicle of the Kings of Castile,* does not appear in the text, but rather was assigned to it by Cirot.

I have attempted to provide the reader with a faithful translation. At times I have the sense that our author wrote in haste and did not always express himself as clearly as he might. The lack of punctuation in the manuscript often makes it difficult to determine the author's meaning; to some extent

Charlo Brea remedied that problem. The author is not always clear when he speaks of more than one king, for example, the king of Castile, or the king of León, and that may confuse the reader. I have broken up long sentences into shorter ones that make more sense. In the notes I have attempted to identify everyone mentioned, insofar as that is possible, and I have also tried to provide the location of the many places cited. In that regard the reader can consult the maps provided with this translation. For a date given in the Spanish era, I have placed in square brackets the date according to the Christian era, which is thirty-eight years earlier; for example: era 1260 [A.D. 1222]. The several lacunae in the text (chaps. 32, 53, 56, 65, 69) are also marked by square brackets. Charlo Brea identified many biblical citations which I have noted, using the text of the *New American Bible* (*NAB*) except where otherwise specified.[57]

---

[57] As the numeration of the Psalms in *NAB* is often one digit ahead of the Vulgate and Douay versions, I have noted this as follows: Psalms 76(75):9.

I. From Count Fernán González to King Sancho III (923–1158)

1. THE GENEALOGY OF THE COUNTS OF CASTILE (923–1065)

After the death of Count Fernán González, the first to hold the countship of Castile[1] (after the destruction wreaked on the Christian people of the Spains[2] in the time of Rodrigo, King of the Goths),[3] his son Count García Fernández succeeded him. He was succeeded by his son Count Sancho whose son, Infante García, was killed at León by some Leonese when he went to marry the daughter of the king or of a certain count.[4]

Count Sancho's surviving daughter, Lady Mayor, was given in marriage to the king of Navarre and Nájera, Sancho by name, a grandson of Sancho Abarca. By Mayor, King Sancho had two sons, namely, García and Fernando, who fought

---

[1] Fernán González (923–970), the hero of the early thirteenth-century epic *Poema de Fernán González* (ed. Alonso Zamora Vicente, Clásicos Castellanos [Madrid: Espasa-Calpe, 1946]), effected the independence of the county of Castile from the kingdom of León. He was succeeded as Count of Castile by his son García Fernández (970–995), his grandson Sancho García (995–1017), and his great-grandson García Sánchez (1017–1029), who was assassinated as he prepared to marry Sancha, the sister of King Vermudo III of León (1038–1037). See O'Callaghan, *Medieval Spain*, 122–130; Manuel Márquez Sterling, *Fernán González. The Man and the Legend* (Oxford, Miss.: University of Mississippi Press, 1980).

[2] This usage recalls the Roman division of Spain into two provinces: Hispania Citerior and Hispania Ulterior (Hither and Further Spain).

[3] Rodrigo, the last Visigothic king of Spain (710–711), was defeated at the Guadalete river on 19 July 711 by the Muslims who then subjugated the Iberian peninsula. See O'Callaghan, *Medieval Spain*, 51–54; Collins, *The Arab Conquest of Spain*, 28–36.

[4] Count García was assassinated by members of the Vela family, namely Bernardo, Nepociano, and Rodrigo.

near Atapuerca where King García was killed.[5] As a result King Fernando had his own kingdom [of Castile] and his brother's kingdom [of Navarre] and also the kingdom of León, because he had married the daughter of Vermudo, king of León.[6]

---

[5] Sancho III, el Mayor or the Great, king of Navarre (1000–1035), the grandson of Sancho II Garcés (or Sancho Abarca), king of Navarre (970–994), married Mayor, the daughter of Count Sancho García of Castile. They had three sons: García III Sánchez, king of Navarre (1035–1054); Fernando I, king of Castile and León (1035–1065), and Ramiro I, king of Aragón (1035–1063). Nájera, a Castilian town, about fifteen miles east of Logroño, was claimed by the kings of Navarre. The battle of Atapuerca, about thirteen miles northeast of Burgos, was fought on 15 September 1054. See Justo Pérez de Urbel, *Sancho el Mayor de Navarra* (Madrid: Diputación Foral de Navarra, 1955), and O'Callaghan, *Medieval Spain*, 134–136; also Stemmata 1 and 2.

[6] As a result of his victory in the battle of Atapuerca Fernando I recovered La Bureba (about thirty miles northeast of Burgos) from Navarre, but that kingdom passed into the hands of Sancho IV Garcés (1054–1076), the son of García III. Fernando I acquired the kingdom of Castile by his marriage to Sancha, the daughter of Alfonso V of León (999–1028) and the sister of Vermudo III of León. After defeating and killing Vermudo III in the battle of Tamarón on 4 September 1037, Fernando I annexed the kingdom of León to his dominions. León and Castile remained united under one ruler until 1157. See Bernard F. Reilly, *The Contest of Christian and Muslim Spain, 1031–1157* (Oxford: Blackwell, 1992), 26–28.

2. Alfonso VI, King of León-Castile (1065–1109)

Upon the death of King Fernando (who was nicknamed the Fat and who liberated Coimbra from the hands of the Moors),[1] his three sons succeeded him in the kingdom: King Sancho in Castile; King Alfonso in León, Asturias, and Galicia; and King García in Nájera and Navarre.[2]

But King Sancho, an energetic and warlike man, was unwilling to share his father's kingdom, as the saying has it, no authority will endure a rival.[3] He seized his brother King García, who died not long after in captivity;[4] he also expelled from his kingdom his brother King Alfonso, who went into exile to the king of the Moors then ruling at Toledo. But, believing that nothing had been done

---

[1] The *Chronicle* refers to Fernando I as *Pinguis*, a word meaning "fat," although he is usually called *el Magno* or the Great; he captured Coimbra on 25 July 1064. See Reilly, *The Contest of Christian and Muslim Spain*, 35–42, and O'Callaghan, *Medieval Spain*, 194–200.

[2] Sancho II of Castile (1065–1072); Alfonso VI of León (1065–1109). Our author erroneously identified the third brother, García (1065–1071) as king of Navarre; in fact he was allotted Galicia. The kingdom of Navarre was ruled at that time by Sancho IV Garcés.

[3] Lucan, *Bellum civile*, 1.92–93: ". . . omnisque potestas / impatiens consortis erit. The author gives the citation ut XXIII q. VII. c. quod aut circa principium . . . erit." Cirot, 20, n. 2.3, remarked: "*Principium* [beginning] is understood well enough, but not what precedes it, which must be a reference." Cabanes Pecourt, *Crónica latina*, 16, n. 2, remarked that "the manuscript says '*XXIII q. VII c.*' which makes no sense." Charlo Brea did not interpret the passage, except to cite Cabanes Pecourt's 1985 effort at interpretation as "23 years 7 months." My friend, the distinguished historian of medieval canon law, Professor James A. Brundage of the University of Kansas, kindly responded to my query (e-mail, 6 January 1999) and pointed out that the author was referring to Gratian's *Decretum*, C. 23 q. 7 c. 3 (*Corpus Iuris Canonici*, 2d ed., ed. E. Friedberg [Leipzig: Tauchnitz, 1879; repr. Graz: Akademische Druck- und Verlagsanstalt, 1995], 1:951–952: "The canon begins with the words '*Quod autem*' and '*principium*' simply means that he's talking about the opening words of the canon, rather than the whole thing. This canon is a selection from St. Augustine's *Epist.* 185.35, addressed to Boniface and dated in 417. The subject is the unjust possession of church property by heretics. The citation does rather suggest that whoever wrote the passage had a pretty good grounding in canon law. It's not the sort of thing one would be apt to pick up casually." The chronicler seems to imply that Sancho II believed that his brothers held power unjustly.

[4] Dispossessed in 1072, García, king of Galicia, recovered his liberty after the assassination of Sancho II later in the year, but he was then imprisoned by Alfonso VI in 1073 and died eighteen years later.

while something remained to be done,[5] King Sancho besieged Zamora, held by his sister Urraca; there, as the report had it, he was killed treacherously by a certain agent of Satan named Vellido Adólfez.[6]

Upon his death the king's sister sent her messengers to her brother King Alfonso, who resided at that time in Toledo. After receiving the messenger the king quickly returned and, by God's disposition, obtained the whole of his father's realm.[7]

The Lord God[8] inspired him with the salutary counsel to besiege Toledo, whose situation he knew very well because, while he had lived there, he had carefully scrutinized its innermost and most secret places. For many years therefore he prudently attacked it, laying waste its crops and destroying all its fruits every year. At length, compelled by the power of God, the Toledan Moors surrendered their city to King Alfonso, honorably receiving him as lord and king, on condition that he allow them to remain in the city, retaining their houses and possessions and serving him as king.[9] After taking the very noble and well-fortified city of Toledo, the king, a wise and powerful man, began to devastate the whole region called Extremadura, and, through the power of our Lord Jesus Christ, ripped from the hands of the Saracens[10] many castles and other towns in the Trasierra.[11]

---

[5] Lucan, *Bellum civile*, 2.657: "nil actum credens cum quid superesset agendum." This passage also appears in *Codex Iustinianus*, 6.35.11.3 and may be another indication of the chronicler's legal training. Alfonso took refuge with the petty king of Toledo, al-Ma'mûn (1043–1075).

[6] Sancho II defeated Alfonso VI at Llantada in 1068 and again at Golpejera in January 1072, and thus reunited the kingdoms of Castile, León, and Galicia under his own rule. He was assassinated on 6 October 1072. O'Callaghan, *Medieval Spain*, 198–200; Reilly, *The Contest of Christian and Muslim Spain*, 40–42.

[7] Alfonso VI now ruled León, Castile, and Galicia. See Bernard F. Reilly, *The Kingdom of León-Castilla under King Alfonso VI, 1065–1109* (Princeton: Princeton University Press, 1988).

[8] Cirot and Cabanes Pecourt read *Dominus Deus*; Charlo Brea, *Dominus*.

[9] Toledo, the ancient seat of the Visigothic kings, now ruled by al-Qadir (1075–1085), surrendered on 6 May 1085: O'Callaghan, *Medieval Spain*, 204–207; Reilly, *Alfonso VI*, 160–184; Lomax, *The Reconquest of Spain*, 52–67.

[10] The phrase "eripiens de manibus sarracenorum" is reminiscent of statements by the canonists to the effect that the Spaniards were creating their own empire by ripping it from the hands of the Saracens. Their intention was to emphasize that the Hispanic empire was *sui generis* and in no way dependent on the Holy Roman Empire. See Gaines Post, *Studies in Medieval Legal Thought. Public Law and the State, 1100–1322* (Princeton: Princeton University Press, 1964), 482–493. Cf. Psalms 30:16, 70:4, 81:4, and 143:11.

4

After thus expanding his realm many times over, the king, because he had no son (for his only son named Sancho, had been killed by the Saracens near the town of Uclés),[12] began to consider and to inquire diligently concerning the man to whom, saving his honor, he could give in marriage his daughter Urraca (whom he had by a legitimate wife).[13] But as he found no one in the Spains whom he deemed worthy to be a royal son-in-law, he summoned from the region of Burgundy (near the river Arar commonly called the Saone) a noble man, vigorous in arms, widely renowned and adorned with good habits, namely, Count Raymond, to whom he joined his daughter Urraca in marriage.[14] The count did not live for a long time thereafter with his wife; he had a son by her, called Alfonso, who later reigned for a long time in the Spains and was called emperor.[15]

One of Count Raymond's relatives, Henry by name, who was also a count, came with him. King Alfonso, out of love for his son-in-law, gave him [Henry] as a wife another daughter (whom he had not had by a legitimate marriage).[16]

---

[11] Extremadura is the region south of the Duero river; Trasierra (*ultra serram* in the Latin text) lies to the south of the mountain ranges of Guadarrama and Gredos.

[12] Alfonso VI's son, Sancho, born in 1093 to the Moorish princess Zaida (the daughter-in-law of al-Mu'tamid, king of Seville), was killed on 29 May 1108 in the battle of Uclés (about sixty-five miles east of Toledo). Reilly believes that Alfonso VI took Zaida as a concubine in order to emphasize his intention to defend Seville against the threat of the Almoravids, a Moroccan sect, who invaded Spain and inflicted a major defeat on the king of León at Zalaca on 23 October 1086. Our author says nothing of the Almoravid invasion. See Reilly, *Alfonso VI*, 234–235, 348–350.

[13] Urraca was Alfonso VI's daughter (and only surviving child) by his second wife, Constance of Burgundy, daughter of Duke Robert the Elder, whom he married in 1079. Our author's comment that she was the king's legitimate wife suggests that he may have known that Infante Sancho was the son of the Moorish princess Zaida, whom the king finally married in March 1106, after the death of his fourth wife, Elizabeth. Zaida was baptized a Christian and took the name Elizabeth. See Reilly, *The Contest of Christian and Muslim Spain*, 96.

[14] Count Raymond of Burgundy, the nephew of Duke Eudes of Burgundy, was betrothed to Urraca in 1087.

[15] Raymond of Burgundy died in September 1107. His son by Urraca was Alfonso Raimúndez, born on 1 March 1105; the future Alfonso VII; he crowned himself Emperor of León in 1135; thereafter medieval Spanish historians consistently refer to him as the *imperator* or emperor.

[16] Sometime before 1096 Count Henry of Burgundy, a cousin of Count Raymond, married Teresa, one of the king's two illegitimate daughters by Jimena Muñoz; the other daughter, Elvira, married Count Raymond IV of Toulouse.

By her Count Henry had a son, namely King Afonso of Portugal, who was the father of King Sancho, the father of King Afonso. Both of them died, suffering under the burden of melancholy.[17]

While the king who had conquered Toledo was still alive, his son-in-law, Count Raymond, died; his son Alfonso, a tender boy, who was later emperor, survived him and was reared in Galicia.[18]

---

[17] The kings of Portugal mentioned were Afonso I Henriquez (1128–1185), Sancho I (1185–1211), and Afonso II (1211–1223); the author wrote this section of the *Chronicle* during the reign of Afonso II. "Both of them died" no doubt refers to Counts Raymond and Henry of Burgundy. What the chronicler meant by *malanconia* or melancholy is not at all clear. Other sources do not mention it.

[18] Raymond of Burgundy died in September 1107. His son, Alfonso Raimúndez, was entrusted to the guardianship of Count Pedro Froilaz, head of the Trastámara family of Galicia, and Bishop, later Archbishop, Diego Gelmírez of Santiago de Compostela.

3. URRACA, QUEEN OF LEÓN-CASTILE (1109–1126)

On the death of King Alfonso, the conqueror of Toledo,[1] his daughter Queen Urraca succeeded him in the kingdom, which she later governed so badly.[2] After her father's death, she married Alfonso, king of Aragón,[3] son of King Sancho who had died while besieging Huesca. His son Pedro succeeded to the kingdom and continued the siege of the town.[4] By the grace of God he captured it, after defeating the king of Zaragoza and a multitude of Saracens in a battle fought on the field of Alcoraz near Huesca.[5]

As King Pedro did not leave any surviving children, Alfonso, king of Aragón (whom, as I mentioned, Queen Urraca married) succeeded to his father's kingdom. She despised him, however, and left him, turning to other affairs, unworthy of relation.[6]

---

[1] Alfonso VI died on 1 July 1109.

[2] See Bernard F. Reilly, *The Kingdom of León-Castilla under Queen Urraca, 1109–1126* (Princeton: Princeton University Press, 1982).

[3] The marriage probably took place in early October 1109.

[4] The kings of Aragón, like those of León-Castile were descended from Sancho III, the Great, of Navarre. They were: Ramiro I (1035–1063), Sancho I Ramírez (1063–1094); Pedro I (1094–1104) who was succeeded by his brother Alfonso I (1104–1134), known as *el Batallador*, the Battler. See Stemma 2.

[5] Sancho I Ramírez was killed on 4 June 1094 during the siege of the Muslim town of Huesca (about fifty miles northeast of Zaragoza). His son Pedro I, after defeating al-Musta'in, the king of Zaragoza, at Alcoraz on 18 November, captured Huesca on 27 November 1096. See Reilly, *The Contest of Christian and Muslim Spain*, 105–115.

[6] Urraca's marriage to Alfonso I in October 1109 was notoriously unhappy and was dissolved by Pope Paschal II on the grounds of consanguinity (they were both great-grandchildren of Sancho III, the Great, of Navarre) in 1110; however, not until 1114 did they terminate their relationship. As a consequence, the potential union of León-Castile-Aragón envisioned by Alfonso VI when he arranged the marriage came to naught. The chronicler may have deemed the queen's affair with Pedro González de Lara unworthy of relation. See Reilly, *Urraca*, 45–118; O'Callaghan, *Medieval Spain*, 216–217.

4. ALFONSO I, KING OF ARAGÓN (1104–1134)

Now at that time, Alfonso, king of Aragón, inwardly touched by sorrow of soul,[1] entered Castile with a host of armed men and inflicted many evils on the kingdom of Castile. His men held many fortresses and many castles in the kingdom of Castile, which the queen indeed had ceded to the king himself.[2] Consequently a great disturbance and a very ruinous war lasting a long time took place throughout the whole kingdom of Castile.

The Castilians, joining Count Gómez, known as Candespina (who was overly familiar with the queen, beyond what was proper), fought against King Alfonso near Sepúlveda; there he defeated them and the count was killed.[3] Then the queen received into her closest intimacy Count Pedro de Lara (father of Count Manrique, Count Nuño, and Count Álvaro); by her he is said to have had a son called Fernando Furtado.[4]

Meanwhile, King Alfonso of Aragón, through his lieutenants and at times by himself, laid waste the kingdom of Castile, wretchedly devastating the whole realm, now deprived of a legitimate defender. The son of Queen Urraca and Count Raymond, namely Alfonso (who afterward was called emperor), had not yet reached the age of puberty and was being reared in Galicia. At last the Castilians, together with the Galicians and Leonese, joined in counsel against the king of Aragón. Bringing Queen Urraca's son, Alfonso, now a young man, from Gali-

---

[1] Genesis 6:6: "When the Lord saw how great was man's wickedness on earth . . . his heart was grieved."

[2] Several truces (1117, 1120, 1123) between Urraca and Alfonso I left him in effective control of La Rioja and the eastern sector of Castile. See Reilly, *The Contest of Christian and Muslim Spain*, 134–141.

[3] Count Gómez González belonged to the noble family of Lara, who figure so prominently in Castilian affairs in the twelfth and thirteenth centuries. The battle of Candespina from which he received his sobriquet took place on 26 October 1111. Sepúlveda is about thirty miles northeast of Segovia.

[4] Count Pedro González de Lara fathered two children by Urraca: Fernando Pérez and Elvira Pérez. Manrique, Nuño, and Álvaro de Lara played prominent roles in Castilian politics in the second half of the twelfth century (see below chap. 9). Rodrigo Jiménez de Rada, *Historia de rebus Hispanie sive Historia Gothica*, ed. Juan Fernández Valverde, Corpus Christianorum Continuatio Mediaevalis 72 (Turnhout: Brepols, 1987), 221–222, Bk. 7, chap. 2, noted that Gómez de Candespina "secretly (*furtive*) sired by the queen a son named Fernando Furtado." The sobriquet Furtado probably alluded to Fernando's illegitimate birth. See Simon Barton, *The Aristocracy in Twelfth-Century León and Castile* (Cambridge: Cambridge University Press, 1997).

cia, they prepared to fight against the king of Aragón. In view of this, the king, knowing that he had no just cause for war against the legitimate lord of the land, left the kingdom and returned to his own realm.[5]

Now this king was a warlike and high-spirited man who fought many battles, and was victorious in them, and inflicted many injuries upon the Saracens.[6] In the end, he besieged the town of Fraga near Lérida. There, not by the power of the Saracens, but rather by their deceit and with God's permission, he is said to have been killed by the Moors, when an unexpected host of Saracens sallied forth from the town which had admitted them unbeknownst to the king and his army.[7] Others are of the opinion that he had escaped from that disaster, though the greater part of his army was destroyed by enemy swords, as is attested by the pile of bones that even today appears to the eyes of beholders in a certain church in the town of Fraga.[8]

After the passage of many years he was said to have come into Aragón in our times. As soon as he came there he was honorably received by the nobles and by King Alfonso, son of the count of Barcelona, as one who was truly known to them by the many signs and secrets he pointed out to the old men who had known him.[9] At the same time another man appeared in Castile, falsely pretend-

---

[5] Alfonso Raimúndez, Urraca's son by Raymond of Burgundy, was proclaimed as Alfonso VII (1126–1157) after her death on 8 March 1126. He set out to recover Burgos, Carrión, Soria, and other Castilian strongholds still in the hands of Alfonso I, whom he met on the battlefield at Támara on 31 July 1127; but war was averted and Alfonso I agreed to yield the places claimed by Alfonso VII as king of Castile.

[6] Alfonso I's most notable triumph was his conquest of Zaragoza on 18 December 1118, which extended his frontier to the Ebro river. In the fall of 1125 he marched through the heart of Muslim Spain, defeating the enemy near Granada, and making his return to Aragón early in the next year. See O'Callaghan, *Medieval Spain*, 218–222.

[7] After taking Mequinenza on the Ebro river (about twenty-five miles south of Lérida) in 1133, the king besieged Fraga (about fifteen miles southwest of Lérida), but he was routed by the Muslims on 17 July 1134. He died later in the summer, on 7 September. See Reilly, *The Contest of Christian and Muslim Spain*, 159–173; Lomax, *The Reconquest of Spain*, 82–86.

[8] It would seem that our author had visited the church of Fraga.

[9] Rodrigo Jiménez de Rada, *Historia de rebus Hispanie*, 223–224, Bk. 7, chap. 3, affirmed that a man claiming to be Alfonso I was hanged by Alfonso II of Aragón (1162–1196), the son of Count Ramon Berenguer IV of Barcelona. The phrase "our times" indicates that our author was writing at least in the second half of the twelfth century. Cf. the reference to "Alfonso, our glorious and famous lord," below chap. 8.

ing, however, to be King Sancho, son of the emperor, and father of our lord, the most illustrious King Alfonso; but both the one in Castile and the one in Aragón ended their days with a miserable death.

After that terrible slaughter near Fraga and after the death of the king (if indeed he died there), because he left no children, the Aragonese, deprived of the comfort and rule of a king, brought out of the monastery a certain Ramiro, the king's brother, a monk and a priest, as the story has it, whom they compelled to take a wife. This he did; by her he had a daughter, whom the count of Barcelona later took to wife, with the result that that county was united to the kingdom of Aragón until the present time. Ramiro, however, after the birth of his daughter, thinking himself useless for the government of the realm, returned to his monastery. But enough of this.[10]

---

[10] By his will of 4 September 1134 Alfonso I left his kingdoms of Aragón and Navarre to the Military Orders of the Temple and the Hospital and the canons of the Holy Sepulchre in Jerusalem. Ramiro II (1134–1137) had been a monk in the monastery of San Pedro de Huesca; responding to the plea of the Aragonese he assumed the royal title and married Agnes of Poitiers, the daughter of Duke William IX of Aquitaine, by whom he had a daughter named Petronila in August 1136. Once she was betrothed on 11 August 1137 to Count Ramon Berenguer IV of Barcelona, Ramiro II, having done his political duty, returned to his monastery where he died in 1158. Agnes returned to France. Ramon Berenguer assumed the government of the kingdom, calling himself Prince of Aragón. His son by Petronila, Alfonso II (1162–1196), succeeded not only to the throne of Aragón but also to the County of Barcelona. The Navarrese, in the meantime, proclaimed García IV Ramírez (1134–1150) as their king. See Reilly, *The Contest of Christian and Muslim Spain,* 181–190; Elena Lourie, "The Will of Alfonso I 'el Batallador,' King of Aragon and Navarre: A Reassessment," and eadem, "The Will of Alfonso I of Aragon and Navarre: A Reply to Dr. Forey," in eadem, *Crusade and Colonisation. Muslims, Christians and Jews in Medieval Aragon* (London: Variorum, 1990), nos. III–IV.

5. ALFONSO VII, EMPEROR OF SPAIN AND KING OF LEÓN–CASTILE (1126–1157)

The beginning of the reign of King Alfonso, who later was hailed as emperor, the son of Count Raymond and Queen Urraca, was insecure; but better fortune followed, for divine grace, "in whose hand are all powers and all the rights of kingdoms,"[1] favored him.[2] For many years he held in peace the whole of Galicia, Asturias, the kingdom of León, as well as Castile, Extremadura, and the Trasierra; he inflicted many injuries upon the Saracens, capturing Córdoba, Baeza, Andújar, and Montoro, and seizing many other castles and towns in those regions.[3] He also took Almería. Though he was fortunate in its acquisition he was less successful in retaining it.[4] The land was silent and at peace in his days;[5] his kingdom was enriched and increased.

When he received the crown of empire and was proclaimed emperor throughout the whole world,[6] the king of Navarre, García Ramírez, son of Infante

---

[1] This is a direct quotation from the prayer for the emperor in the Good Friday liturgy: "Omnipotens sempiterne Deus, in cuius manu sunt omnium potestates et omnia jura regnorum." Cf. Sirach 10:4: "Sovereignty over the earth is in the hand of God."

[2] See Bernard F. Reilly, *The Kingdom of León–Castilla under King Alfonso VII, 1126–1157* (Philadelphia: University of Pennsylvania Press, 1998).

[3] Taking advantage of confusion accompanying the disintegration of the Almoravid empire, Alfonso VII temporarily occupied Córdoba, one of the principal cities of Andalucía, in May 1146, and then briefly entered Úbeda, Baeza, and Andújar (all situated in the Guadalquivir valley about forty to eighty miles east of Córdoba). Early in the new year the Almohads invaded Spain and established control of all these places. Alfonso VII's one permanent conquest at this time was Calatrava la vieja (later the seat of the Military Order of Calatrava), which was taken on 9 January 1147. See Reilly, *Alfonso VII*, 90–95; O'Callaghan, *Medieval Spain,* 227–229.

[4] Aided by Ramon Berenguer IV of Barcelona and a Genoese fleet, Alfonso VII besieged the port of Almería, about seventy miles southeast of Granada, on 1 August 1147; the city surrendered on 17 October. The Almohads, after establishing their dominance over southwestern Andalucía, seized Málaga in 1153 and Granada in 1154 and then advanced on Almería; despite Alfonso VII's efforts to come to the rescue, Almería fell to the Almohads in 1157. See Reilly, *Alfonso VII*, 93–100, 131–134; O'Callaghan, *Medieval Spain,* 231–232; Lomax, *The Reconquest of Spain,* 86–91.

[5] 1 Maccabees 1:3: "The earth fell silent before him"; Psalms 76(75):9: "The earth feared and was silent"; and cf. Habakkuk, 2:20.

[6] Alfonso VII was crowned as emperor in the cathedral of León on Pentecost Sunday, 26 May 1135. See Reilly, *Alfonso VII*, 45–50; O'Callaghan, *Medieval Spain,* 222–224.

Ramiro (who was the son by a certain lady of Infante Sancho, son of King García, who was killed at Atapuerca), is said to have been his vassal.[7] The Count of Barcelona, whose sister Berenguela the emperor married, was also a vassal of the emperor for those lands located near the Ebro river in the kingdom of Aragón.[8]

---

[7] García IV Ramírez, king of Navarre (1134–1150), was the son of Infante Ramiro, son of Infante Sancho, son of García III Sánchez (1035–1054). See Stemma 2

[8] Alfonso VII married Berenguela, the daughter of Ramon Berenguer III, count of Barcelona, and the sister of Ramon Berenguer IV, in November 1127: Reilly, *Alfonso VII*, 20–21.

6. THE COMING OF THE ALMOHADS

Around the beginning of the emperor's reign a certain Saracen named Ibn Tûmart appeared.[1] Coming from the region of the noble and famous city of Baghdad where he had studied for a long time, he preached in the kingdom of Morocco, then held by the Moors who were known by the special name Moabites (who are commonly called Almoravids). The name of their king was 'Alî.[2]

Now he preached especially against the arrogance and oppression of the Moabites who cruelly repressed the people subject to them, frequently imposing excessive exactions, in order to practice as they wished the vice of their liberality, nay rather, prodigality, in which they labored and gloried. Thus he drew to himself innumerable people who, anxious to cast off from their necks the yoke of a very harsh servitude, willingly followed him. As a wise and discreet man, even though an infidel, he won to himself the minds of men, promising them the inestimable gift of liberty. Now among those who followed Ibn Tûmart was a discreet, generous, and warlike man named 'Abd al-Mu'min, whose services he often used in difficult tasks.[3] For Ibn Tûmart and his followers fought against the king of the Moabites and against the people; though often defeated by the Moabites, they conquered them at last and expelled them from the kingdom, and occupied the famous city of Marrakech.[4]

Then 'Abd al-Mu'min was established as king in that city and in the kingdom of the Moabites by the hand of Ibn Tûmart,[5] who was, as it were, his prophet.

---

[1] Abû 'Abd Allâh Ibn Tûmart (d. 1130), a native of Morocco, made a pilgrimage to Mecca and studied in Baghdad with the famous philosopher al-Ghazzâlî. Returning to Morocco, he denounced the corruption of the Almoravid regime and the rigidity of the Malikite jurists who dominated the thought of Spanish and Moroccan Islam. Proclaiming himself the *mahdî*, the rightly-guided one, descended from the Prophet, who would come at the end of time to render justice and to secure the final triumph of Islam, he waged a holy war against the Almoravids. See Kennedy, *Muslim Spain and Portugal*, 196–199; O'Callaghan, *Medieval Spain*, 227–228.

[2] 'Alî (1106–1143) succeeded his father Yûsuf ibn Tashufin (1061–1106) as the Almoravid emir of the Muslims. On the Almoravids and the Almohads who followed them see Fletcher, *Moorish Spain*, 105–130; Lomax, *The Reconquest of Spain*, 68–80, 91–93.

[3] 'Abd al-Mu'min, the first caliph of the Almohads, ruled from 1130 to 1163: Kennedy, *Muslim Spain and Portugal*, 200–215.

[4] After dispossessing Tashufin ibn 'Alî (1143–1145), the last Almoravid emir, the Almohads occupied Oran and Tlemcen, and in 1147 took Fez and Marrakech.

[5] Ibn Tûmart had died in 1130.

Now those who won the kingdom in this way were called Almohads, that is, Unitarians, because they devoted themselves to the cult of one God whom Ibn Tûmart preached, as is set forth clearly in a certain book that he wrote.[6] From 'Abd al-Mu'min are descended those who, up to the present time, have held the kingdom of Morocco which has flourished from then until now. But now by the power of our Lord Jesus Christ, it is wonderfully beginning to be destroyed.[7]

'Abd al-Mu'min's son was Abû Ya'qûb who died in Portugal when he laid siege to the noble and famous town of Santarém.[8] His son fought the battle of Alarcos and, with God's permission, gained the victory over the Christians, capturing Calatrava, Alarcos, and other castles nearby, as well as Malagón and the tower of Guadalerzas. Of this king and his deeds more will be said later, but enough of this now.[9]

---

[6] Ibn Tûmart called his followers *al-muwahhidûn* or Almohads, a name emphasizing their belief in the absolute unity (*tawhid*) of God; hence they were known as Unitarians. Whatever the book may have been, it does not appear to be extant.

[7] This passage indicates that the author was witnessing the collapse of the Almohad empire in the first half of the thirteenth century.

[8] Abû Ya'qûb Yûsuf (1163–1184) invaded Spain in the spring of 1184 and besieged Santarém (about forty-five miles north of Lisbon), but Afonso I Henriques of Portugal, aided by Fernando II of León, forced him to withdraw. The caliph was wounded and died on 29 July 1184 on his return to Seville. See Kennedy, *Muslim Spain and Portugal,* 235–236; O'Callaghan, *Medieval Spain,* 241.

[9] Ya'qûb ibn Abû Ya'qûb was proclaimed as caliph on 30 July 1184 and ruled until 1199. He took the honorific name al-Mansûr, the Victorious. See below, chaps. 12–13, for the battle of Alarcos and its sequel.

7. ALFONSO VII'S SEPARATION OF CASTILE AND LEÓN

Louis, king of the French, took to wife the emperor's daughter named Sancha.[1]

His [Alfonso VII's] two sons harmed the emperor's kingdom, and this was the cause of the many slayings and many evils that happened in the Spains. For, with God's permission, because of the sins of men, at the instigation of Fernando, Count of Galicia, he divided his realm between his two sons. To Sancho, the first-born, he gave Castile, Ávila, Segovia, and other nearby towns in Extremadura, and Toledo, and all of Trasierra in those regions, as well as the Tierra de Campos as far as Sahagún and Asturias de Santillana.[2] But he gave the rest of his kingdom as far as León and Galicia, Toro, Zamora, and Salamanca, with other adjacent towns, to his younger son, Fernando.[3] After this unhappy division, when the emperor was returning from the land of the Saracens with his army, he died near the Puerto del Muradal, and was buried in the cathedral of Toledo.[4]

---

[1] Alfonso VII's daughter Sancha was betrothed to Sancho VI, king of Navarre, in June 1153. About the same time the French king, Louis VII (1137–1180), who had just divorced his first wife, Eleanor of Aquitaine, married Alfonso VII's daughter Constanza; but the marriage ended when she failed to give him a male heir; she returned to León in 1156. See Reilly, *Alfonso VII*, 118–119.

[2] Sancho III (1157–1158) received Castile. The Tierra de Campos was the territory in the modern provinces of Palencia and Valladolid. The monastery and town of Sahagún was on the border between Castile and León, about thirty miles southeast of the city of León. Asturias de Santillana referred to the coastal region along the Bay of Biscay, generally the modern province of Santander.

[3] Fernando II (1157–1188) received the kingdom of León. See Julio González, *Regesta de Fernando II* (Madrid: Consejo superior de Investigacions científicas, 1943).

[4] Alfonso VII died on 21 August 1157 at Almuradiel (about forty miles southeast of Ciudad Real) after failing to relieve Almería, which fell to the Almohads. The Puerto del Muradal (modern Despeñaperros) gives access through the Sierra Morena. See Reilly, *Alfonso VII*, 127–134; O'Callaghan, *Medieval Spain*, 232–233.

8. SANCHO III, KING OF CASTILE (1157–1158)

His son, King Sancho, before his father's death, had married Lady Blanca, daughter of García Ramírez, king of Navarre; before the emperor's death he had a son by her, namely, Alfonso [VIII], our glorious and famous lord. King Sancho undertook many difficult and remarkable tasks at the beginning of his reign, so that all who knew him expected that because of those things that he had previously accomplished and that he had recently undertaken, he would be a powerful king. But the Most High, who disposes all things,[1] ended his life a year after his father's death. He was buried near his father in the cathedral of Toledo.[2]

---

[1] Wisdom 8:1: "Indeed, she [Wisdom] reaches from end to end mightily and governs all things well."

[2] Sancho III, born around 1133, married Blanca, the daughter of García IV Ramírez of Navarre, on 30 January 1151 in Calahorra. Their son, Alfonso VIII, was born on 11 November 1155. Blanca died on 12 August 1156, and Sancho III died on 31 August 1158 and was buried in the cathedral of Toledo. See O'Callaghan, *Medieval Spain*, 234–235.

II. The Reign of Alfonso VIII,
King of Castile (1158–1214)

9. THE MINORITY OF ALFONSO VIII

After his death, his glorious son Alfonso, a tender child scarcely three years old, survived, but there was greater turbulence in the kingdom of Castile than there had been for many long years.[1] The magnates of the realm quarreled among themselves. Fernando Rodríguez (son of Rodrigo Fernández, brother of Gutierre Fernández de Castro),[2] and his brothers and other friends and relations who followed him, formed a party, seeking to escape the persecution and oppression of the sons of Count Pedro de Lara, namely, Count Manrique, Count Nuño, and Count Álvaro and all their relations.[3] Now Fernando Rodríguez and his brothers and relatives held many castles, fortresses, and strongholds in King Sancho's name. At the time of his death he commanded them as well as the other magnates of the realm not to give the lands and castles that they held to anyone except his son, but only when he attained his fifteenth year.

Thus discord and bitter hatred broke out between the factions of nobles mentioned above. Count Manrique and his brother Count Nuño had King Alfonso in

---

[1] Julio González, *El reino de Castilla en la época de Alfonso VIII*, 3 vols. (Madrid: Consejo superior de Investigaciones científicas, 1960), is the major study of the reigns of Sancho III and Alfonso VIII. See also O'Callaghan, *Medieval Spain*, 234–236.

[2] Sancho III had entrusted his son, the child king, to the tutelage of Gutierre Fernández de Castro. His brother, Rodrigo Fernández de Castro, had a son, Fernando Rodríguez de Castro, who was nicknamed *el castellano* (the Castilian) and entered the service of Fernando II of León who appointed him as his *mayordomo*.

[3] Sancho III had appointed Count Manrique Pérez de Lara, the son of Count Pedro González de Lara, as regent for Alfonso VIII; but Count Manrique and his brothers wanted to gain control of the person of the young king and of royal castles held by the Castros in the king's name.

their custody and held the kingdom for a long time. By means of the boy they attempted to subject everything to themselves, as they said, for his honor and utility.[4] But the opposing party, as it is believed, persuaded King Fernando, son of the emperor, to enter the kingdom of Castile; as he was more nearly related to the boy, he wished to have wardship of the boy and custody of the realm. But the counts thwarted him, both by a deception (though praiseworthy) and by force, so that he could not achieve what he desired.[5]

During that time innumerable killings and rapine without measure occurred here and there throughout all parts of the kingdom. At that time Count Manrique fought against Fernando Rodríguez and the people of Huete who were with him; but the count, who had the boy–king with him, was defeated in the battle and was killed in the same battle.[6]

---

[4] By early 1159 Count Manrique had induced Gutierre Fernández de Castro to yield custody of the king to García de Aza, the half-brother of the Lara counts; by the middle of 1160 he handed the king over to Count Manrique.

[5] Urged on by the Castros, Fernando II, king of León, invaded Castile in July 1162 and occupied Toledo on 9 August. By September the Laras acknowledged him as Alfonso VIII's tutor, but in November Fernando II again entrusted the person of the young king to Count Manrique; the latter opposed Fernando II's efforts to assume the regency for Alfonso VIII.

[6] The battle of Huete (about thirty miles west of Cuenca) occurred on 9 July 1164. After Count Manrique's death, his brother, Count Nuño, assumed the regency and soon overcame his opponents. Cirot and Cabanes Pecourt read *regem puerum*, but Charlo Brea reads *puerum*. He does not record these variants in his apparatus.

10. THE MAJORITY AND EARLY CAMPAIGNS OF ALFONSO VIII

When the glorious king reached his fifteenth year,[1] Fernando Rodríguez and his brothers and friends restored to King Alfonso, in accordance with his father's command, the lands and castles that they held. Now a fully grown young man, the king began to act manfully and take comfort in the Lord,[2] and to dispense justice which he always loved and forcefully and wisely administered until the end of his life.[3]

While still a youth he besieged Cuenca, keeping it under siege for a long time; by the grace of God he assaulted and captured it and through his efforts adorned it with the pontifical dignity. Today it is, by nature and art, one of the noblest and strongest cities in the kingdom of Castile.[4] Afterward he recovered Logroño and other towns and castles near Navarre which his uncle King Sancho (his mother's brother) had occupied for a long time.[5] At the same time he led a large and powerful army against his uncle King Fernando of León and recovered the land called Infantazgo.[6]

---

[1] Alfonso VIII reached the age of fourteen on 11 November 1169 and assumed the arms of knighthood from the altar of the monastery of San Zoil in Carrión and then went to Burgos where he celebrated the first curia of his majority.

[2] Joshua 1:18: "Be firm and steadfast"; 1 Chronicles, 22:13: "Be brave and steadfast; do not fear and lose heart", and 28:20: "Be firm and steadfast; go to work without fear or discouragement."

[3] This indicates that the author was writing after 1214.

[4] With the help of Alfonso II of Aragón, Alfonso VIII laid siege to Cuenca (about a hundred miles east of Toledo) and captured it on 14 September 1177. Not only did he establish a bishopric there (the first bishop-elect, Juan, is attested on 10 April 1078), but he also gave the inhabitants a *fuero* or charter which became the model for royal charters given to many of the towns in Andalucía. See James F. Powers's translation of the *fuero*: *The Code of Cuenca. Municipal Law on the Twelfth-Century Castilian Frontier* (Philadelphia: University of Pennsylvania Press, 2000).

[5] During Alfonso VIII's minority Sancho VI of Navarre (1150–1194) had occupied Castilian lands, including Logroño (about fifty miles southwest of Pamplona, the seat of the kings of Navarre). Sancho VI's sister Blanca was the wife of Sancho III of Castile and the mother of Alfonso VIII. The two kings agreed to submit the issue to the arbitration of King Henry II of England, who decided for Castile in 1176. Even so, tension along the frontier continued for many years. See O'Callaghan, *Medieval Spain*, 232, 236, 239–240.

[6] The Infantazgo was so-called because Fernando I had assigned the revenues of the Leonese monasteries to his daughters Urraca and Elvira. Alfonso VIII tried to recover it from about 1179 to 1181.

King Fernando had married Urraca, daughter of King Afonso of Portugal, though she could not be his legitimate wife, because she was related to him in the third degree, according to the canonical reckoning; for the emperor and the king of Portugal, as the sons of two sisters, the daughters of King Alfonso who conquered Toledo, were related to one another in the second degree.[7] On account of this impious union, the king [Fernando] had given the king of Portugal many castles which he later recovered from him, when he was captured at Badajoz and broke his leg, so that he was never able to ride again.[8]

At that time Geraldo, called the Fearless, was also captured and delivered into the hands of Rodrigo Fernández, the Castilian.[9] In return for his liberty Geraldo gave him Montánchez, Trujillo, Santa Cruz, and Monfrag,[10] which Geraldo had

---

[7] Fernando II married Urraca, daughter of Afonso I Henriques of Portugal, in 1165. The problem of consanguinity mentioned by our author (on his interest in canon law see introduction, p. xxxiii) arose because the two kings, as descendants of Alfonso VI of León–Castile, were first cousins once removed; Fernando and Urraca were second cousins:

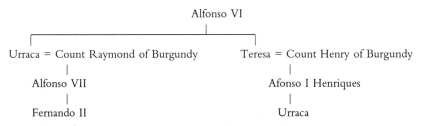

[8] In the years from 1165 to 1168 a Portuguese knight, Geraldo Sempavor, or the Fearless, seized several fortresses in the zone between the Tagus and the Guadiana rivers: Évora, Trujillo, Cáceres, Montánchez, Serpa, and Juromenha. Then on 3 May 1169 he broke into the town of Badajoz (on the Guadiana river) and summoned Afonso I to help him in taking the citadel. Fernando II also advanced against the city because, according to the treaty of Sahagún which he had concluded with his brother, Sancho III, in 1158, the places in question were reserved to Leonese conquest. As Afonso I tried to flee he broke his leg; Fernando II liberated him and his allies in return for the cession of Montánchez, Trujillo, and other places. He allowed the Muslims to retain Badajoz as his vassals, but once he departed they opened the gates to the Almohads. See González, *Fernando II,* 79–81; O'Callaghan, *Medieval Spain,* 237–238; Lomax, *The Reconquest of Spain,* 112–116.

[9] Instead of Rodrigo Fernández, one should read Fernando Rodríguez de Castro, who left Castile and entered the service of Fernando II of León; he died in 1185.

[10] Montánchez is about twenty-five miles southeast, and Trujillo is about the same distance east of Cáceres; Santa Cruz is about ten miles south of Trujillo; Monfrag is on the

seized from the Saracens. Impoverished now and bereft of all help, he went over to the Saracens upon whom he had inflicted many injuries; he was beheaded by them in the land of Morocco, on a minor pretext.[11]

Tagus about ten miles south of Plasencia. In 1221 Fernando III gave the castle of Monfrag to the Order of Calatrava, thereby ending the independent existence of the Military Order of Monfrag. See Joseph F. O'Callaghan, "The Foundation of the Order of Alcántara, 1176–1218," in idem, *The Spanish Military Order of Calatrava and its Affiliates* (London: Variorum, 1975), no. IV. 481–484; Alan Forey, "The Order of Mountjoy," *Speculum* 46 (1971): 250–266.

[11] Geraldo defected to the Almohads, who beheaded him in 1174 on suspicion of conspiring with Afonso I: González, *Fernando II,* 86–88, 101, 107.

11. ALFONSO IX, KING OF LEÓN (1188–1230)

By Urraca already mentioned, King Fernando had a son named Alfonso, who now reigns in his father's place as king of León.[1] On the death of King Fernando,[2] his son, then an adolescent, feared that he would be deprived of his realm by the power of Lord Alfonso, the glorious king of Castile, whose praise and fame had already filled a great part of the world. He was dreaded and feared at that time by all the neighboring kings, both Saracen and Christian.

Thus it was arranged and provided that one of the daughters of the king of Castile should be espoused to King Alfonso of León, though this was contrary to divine and canon laws, since the two kings, as sons of two brothers, were related to one another in the second degree. In addition, it was agreed and confirmed that the king of León should be made a knight by the king of Castile and then that he should kiss his hand. This was done.[3] Now a famous and noble curia was celebrated at Carrión where the king of León was girded with his sword by the king of Castile in the church of San Zoilo. He also kissed the hand of the king of Castile in the presence of Galicians, Leonese, and Castilians.[4]

---

[1] This sentence indicates that this section of the *Chronicle* was written during the lifetime of Alfonso IX.

[2] Fernando II died on 22 January 1188. His son was seventeen. See Julio González, *Alfonso IX*, 2 vols. (Madrid: Consejo superior de Investigaciones científicas, 1945).

[3] The proposed marriage between Alfonso IX and one of Alfonso VIII's daughters evidently did not come off at this time. In 1191 Alfonso IX married his first cousin, Teresa, daughter of King Sancho I of Portugal; under papal pressure they separated in 1194. After many years of conflict with Castile, Alfonso IX married Berenguela, the oldest daughter of Alfonso VIII, at Valladolid in October 1197. Once again our author emphasized the problem of consanguinity, as the two kings were second cousins; moreover, Berenguela was a second cousin once removed of her husband:

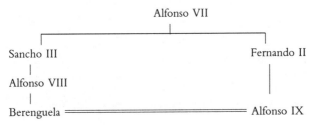

[4] During the curia of Carrión de los Condes (about fifty miles directly west of Burgos) held in June 1188, in the hope of averting conflict with Castile, Alfonso IX was knighted

After a short interval of scarcely two months when a magnificent curia was again celebrated in the same town of Carrión, Conrad, son of Frederick, emperor of the Romans, was made a knight by the king of Castile, who espoused his daughter, Lady Berenguela (who was hardly eight years old) to him. He caused homage to be done to him by the entire realm, so that Conrad should reign after him, if it happened that he should die without a son. For at that time the glorious King Lord Alfonso did not have a son, but only daughters.[5]

---

by Alfonso VIII and kissed his hand as a sign of vassalage, though he ever after regarded that act as a great humiliation. See Joseph F. O'Callaghan, "The Beginnings of the Cortes of León–Castile," *American Historical Review* 74 (1969): 1516, repr. in idem, *Alfonso X, The Cortes, and Government in Medieval Spain* (Aldershot, Hampshire: Ashgate/Variorum, 1998), no. IX; O'Callaghan, *Medieval Spain*, 241–242.

[5] In May 1187 Alfonso VIII celebrated a curia at San Esteban de Gormaz to arrange the betrothal of his daughter Berenguela to Conrad of Hohenstaufen, the son of Emperor Frederick Barbarossa. The marriage contract was signed at Seligenstadt in April 1188. Conrad came to the curia of Carrión in July 1188, where he too was knighted by Alfonso VIII and betrothed to Berenguela, then eight years old. Conrad returned to Germany. The papal legate, Cardinal Gregory, annulled the marriage contract, so that Berenguela was free to marry Alfonso IX in 1197. See O'Callaghan, "The Beginnings of the Cortes of León–Castile," 1512–1513, 1516; González, *Alfonso VIII*, 2:857–863, no. 499.

12. PREPARATIONS FOR THE BATTLE OF ALARCOS

At that time he had already built the famous and opulent city of Plasencia and he had seized from the Saracens the strongly fortified castle named Alarcón.[1] He also began to build the town called Alarcos.[2] But before the wall was completed and the settlers established in that place, he made war on the king of Morocco, whose realm flourished at that time and whose power and great glory was feared by neighboring kings.

For the lord king of Castile sent the archbishop of Toledo, Lord Martín, of happy memory, a discreet, benign, and generous man who was loved so much by everyone that he was considered the father of all.[3] Now the archbishop took with him noble and bold men and a host of knights and foot soldiers with whom he ravaged a goodly part of the land of the Moors on this side of the sea, despoiling it of many riches and a infinite number of cows, sheep, and beasts of burden.[4]

When the king of Morocco (the third from 'Abd al-Mu'min, who was mentioned above) heard of this, he groaned, stricken inwardly with sorrow in his heart.[5] Leaving Morocco at once he gathered an infinite multitude of knights and foot soldiers and crossed the sea. He went to Córdoba and passed through the Puerto del Muradal with great speed, advancing to the plain of the castle now called Salvatierra.[6]

---

[1] Plasencia, situated about one hundred and ten miles west of Toledo and north of the Tagus river, was repopulated around 1188–1189; in 1189 a diocese was established there. The king took Alarcón, about forty miles directly south of Cuenca, in 1184.

[2] Alarcos is situated on the left bank of the Guadiana river, about eight miles west of modern Ciudad Real. The king began to fortify it in 1193.

[3] This sentence suggests that our author knew Archbishop Martín López de Pisuerga (1192–1209), and may have served in the archiepiscopal curia.

[4] In 1194 Alfonso VIII sent Archbishop Martín on an expedition that ravaged Andalucía as far as Seville.

[5] Genesis 6:6: "When the Lord saw how great was man's wickedness on earth . . . his heart was grieved" (quoted above, chap. 4, n. 1). On 'Abd al-Mu'min see chap. 6 above.

[6] The third Almohad caliph was Ya'qûb ibn Abû Ya'qûb Yûsuf, better known by the honorific title al-Mansûr (1184–1199) (cf. above, chap. 6, n. 9). He left Marrakech in Morocco, landed at Tarifa on 1 June 1195 and advanced to Córdoba (30 June); he then moved northward through the Puerto del Muradal (Despeñaperros) into the campo de Calatrava and encamped near El Congosto between the castles of Salvatierra and Alarcos on 13 July. Though it probably had a Muslim name, the name Salvatierra appears in 1194. It was located about twenty miles south of Ciudad Real.

When the glorious King Lord Alfonso heard of the coming of the Moor Mira-mamolín (for the kings of Morocco were so called),[7] he commanded his vassals to follow him with all speed. Like a lion roaring and rampaging before his prey,[8] he set out ahead of his men and came to Toledo in great haste. There he spent a few days awaiting the magnates of the realm and noble vassals and a multitude of people who were following him. Then he advanced to Alarcos where he established a camp, firmly intending (as appeared later) to join battle with Miramamo-lín, if he went past the place called El Congosto toward Alarcos which was considered the beginning of the kingdom of Castile.[9]

For he preferred to expose his life and his kingdom to such a great conflict and to submit to the will of God by fighting against the king of the Moors, who was thought to be more powerful and richer than all the Saracens, rather than to permit that king to enter his kingdom for any distance whatsoever. On this account, although certain prudent men, expert in military affairs, advised him to do so, the glorious king of Castile did not wish to wait for the king of León who was coming to his assistance, and was already active in the district of Talavera. Then the Moor[10] called Miramamolín came to the place called Congosto between the castle of Salvatierra and Alarcos and encamped there.[11]

---

[7] Miramamolín is the Castilian version of the caliphal title *amîr al-mu'minîn*, that is, prince of believers or commander of the faithful. The Almohads, unlike the Almoravids before them, laid claim to the caliphal title.

[8] Ezekiel 22:25: "Her princes are like roaring lions that tear prey."

[9] Alfonso VIII reached Alarcos at the end of June. El Congosto was situated between Salvatierra and Alarcos.

[10] Both Cirot and Charlo Brea in his first edition of the text read: "*Demens igitur dictus Maurus. . . .*" ["the raving Moor"]. Now in his second edition Charlo Brea reads *demens* as *veniens*, which makes sense, but it would not have been unusual for a Christian author to describe Miramamolín as a "raving" Moor.

[11] Alfonso IX had responded to the summons of Alfonso VIII for help, but was still on the road from Talavera to Toledo when the battle took place. The caliph camped at El Congosto on 13 July.

13. THE BATTLE OF ALARCOS, 19 JULY 1195

When he heard this, the glorious king of Castile ordered all his men to advance fully armed into the field early in the morning to give battle to the king of the Moors. For he believed that the king of the Moors would come to the battle that same day.

Thus, when morning broke the Castilians advanced to the field, ready to fight and to brandish their spears against the enemy if they should be there. But the Moors rested that day, preparing themselves for the next day; they hoped thus to avoid their enemies who, wearied on that day from the weight of their arms, and thirsty, would be found less ready for war on the following day. And so it happened. For the glorious king of Castile and his army, thirsty and burdened by the weight of their arms, waited for the enemy on the field from early morning until afternoon, when they returned to their camp, thinking that the king of the Moors did not dare to fight with them.[1]

But around midnight the king of the Moors ordered his men to prepare for battle, and early in the morning they appeared suddenly in the field where the king of Castile had stood the day before. A tumult broke out in the Christian camp and, as so often happens, an unforeseen event caused both wonderment and fear in the enemy [the Christians].[2] Then leaving their tents quickly and in disorder, they advanced to the field and joined battle with the Moors. In the first rank of the Christians great men fell: Ordoño García de Roda and his brothers, Pedro Rodríguez de Guzmán, Rodrigo Sánchez, his son-in-law, and many others.[3]

The Arabs spread far and wide to the destruction of the Christian people. Arrows without number taken from their quivers flew uncertainly through the air, but just as certainly inflicted wounds on the Christians. Both sides fought vigorously. A day prodigal of human blood sent Moors to hell and Christians to eternal mansions.[4]

---

[1] This first challenge by the Christian forces took place on 18 July, but the Almohads opted not to respond at that time.

[2] The battle of Alarcos took place on 19 July 1195: Lomax, *The Reconquest of Spain,* 116–120; Kennedy, *Muslim Spain and Portugal,* 237–246. Ambrosio Huici Miranda, *Las grandes batallas de la reconquista* (Madrid: Consejo superior de Investigaciones científicas, 1956), 137–218 described the battle in detail.

[3] Pedro Rodríguez de Guzmán was the royal *mayordomo;* Ordoño García de Roa and Rodrigo Sánchez are not otherwise identified.

[4] Cf. Prudentius, *Hamartigenia,* 882.

Seeing his men falling in battle, the noble and glorious king rushed forward, manfully throwing himself into the midst of the enemy, and with his followers struck down many Moors on the right and on the left. But his men, who most closely attended upon him, saw that they could not resist the infinite multitude of Moors. For many of their own men had already fallen in the battle — indeed the battle had lasted a long time, and the sun was now shining at midday on the feast of St. Marina [19 July]. They besought him to retreat and to save his life, because the Lord God seemed to be angry with the Christian people. But he was unwilling to listen to them, hoping to end his life with a glorious death rather than to withdraw from the battle in defeat. His men, however, realizing the danger threatening the whole of Spain, led him unwillingly and involuntarily from the battle. Lamenting and bemoaning the great disaster that had happened, he went then to Toledo with a few knights.[5]

His noble vassal, Diego López de Vizcaya, escaped to the castle of Alarcos where the Moors besieged him; but through the grace of God who was reserving him for great things, after giving some hostages, he got away and, following the king, came to Toledo a few days later.[6] The king of the Moors seized the spoils and took certain castles, namely the tower of Guadalerzas, Malagón, Benavente, Calatrava, Alarcos, and Caracuel, and then returned to his own realm.[7]

---

[5] The king was in Toledo at least on 28 July 1195.

[6] Diego López de Haro, lord of Vizcaya, the royal *alférez* or standardbearer; tried to defend Alarcos, but agreed to surrender it, and was able to retreat to Toledo sometime before 27 July.

[7] Guadalerzas lies four miles north of Malagón which is thirteen miles north of Ciudad Real; Benavente is ten miles to the west, and Caracuel, thirteen miles to the southwest. All these castles belonged to the Military Order of Calatrava. The caliph returned to Seville by 7 August. See Joseph F. O'Callaghan, "The Order of Calatrava, 1158–1212: Years of Crisis and Survival," in *The Meeting of Two Worlds. Cultural Exchange between East and West during the Period of the Crusades*, ed. Vladimir P. Goss and Christine Verzár Bornstein (Kalamazoo: Western Michigan University Press, 1986), 421–422.

14. ALFONSO IX OF LEÓN MAKES WAR AGAINST CASTILE

Meanwhile, the king of León who was coming to the aid of the king of Castile came to Toledo; but on the advice of certain agents of Satan, he turned into a crooked bow[1] and looked for reasons to abandon his friend. Once a friend, he now became the cruelest enemy. For he kept in the back of his mind[2] what had happened to him in the curia celebrated at Carrión mentioned above.[3]

Pleased and rejoicing over the misfortune that had befallen the Castilians, he withdrew from Toledo, indignant with the glorious king because he had not given him certain castles that he had demanded.

He immediately allied himself with the king of Morocco, accepting money and a host of armed knights from him, and made war upon the king of Castile. Then in the following year, at that time when kings are accustomed to go to war, together with Miramamolín, he laid waste Trasierra and for many days almost held the city of Toledo under siege.[4] The king of León invaded the kingdom of Castile through the Tierra de Campos with the multitude of Moors already mentioned, who, as enemies of the cross of Christ, committed many enormities upon the churches and ecclesiastical ornaments, to the outrage and dishonor of the Christian religion. He came as far as Carrión where he seemed to purge himself of the dishonor he believed he had suffered when he kissed the hand of the king of Castile.[5]

At the same time, King Sancho of Navarre, who was related to the king of Castile in the second degree of kindred on both sides,[6] built a certain castle called

---

[1] Psalms 78:57: "They proved false like a bow with no tension."

[2] Virgil, *Aeneid* 1:26: "manet alta mente repostum" (metrically incorrectly *repositum* in the Latin text).

[3] See above chap. 11 for the curia of Carrión in 1188.

[4] The caliph, who had returned to Seville after capturing Guadalerzas and the other castles following the battle of Alarcos, began his campaign in June 1196, capturing Montánchez, Santa Cruz, Trujillo, and Plasencia, and then ravaging the lands about Talavera. He then besieged Toledo for ten days. Alfonso VIII recovered Plasencia on 15 August 1196 after the caliph's departure.

[5] The Tierra de Campos was a zone east of the kingdom of León in the modern provinces of Palencia and Valladolid. In the curia of Carrión in 1188 Alfonso IX kissed Alfonso VIII's hand as a sign of homage and fealty (see above chap. 11).

[6] Our author again comments on consanguinity when he notes that Sancho VII of Navarre (1194–1234) and Alfonso VIII were second cousins:

Corvo, near the vineyards of Logroño. He also began to ravage the kingdom of Castile in that area, for he thought he had some just cause for war.

The Christians, thus bound to the Moors in an impious alliance,[7] seemed to have conspired for the ruination of the king of Castile. They atrociously inflicted whatever evils they could throughout the whole kingdom, so much so that nowhere in the entire realm could anyone find a corner in which he could be safe. The fire of the Lord's anger seemed to be raging,[8] and if the noble king had felt any elation of spirit, he now seemed to be cast down from his former glory. The prudent and noble king now understood that the kingdom of the sons of men is in the hand of God who will give it to whomever He wishes.[9]

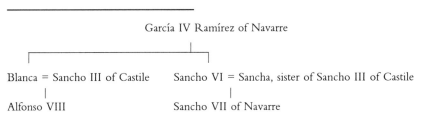

García IV Ramírez of Navarre

Blanca = Sancho III of Castile   Sancho VI = Sancha, sister of Sancho III of Castile

Alfonso VIII   Sancho VII of Navarre

[7] Isaiah 58:6: "colligationes impietatis" ["bands of wickedness"] (Douay).

[8] Psalms 78:21: "The Lord heard and grew angry; fire blazed up against Jacob; anger flared up against Israel." In the Latin text *ascensus* appears erroneously for *accensus*.

[9] Daniel 4:14: "That all who live may know that the Most High rules over the kingdom of men: He can give it to whom he will, or set over it the lowliest of men"; 4:29: "until you learn that the Most High rules over the kingdom of men and gives it to whom he will"; 5:21: "until he learned that the Most High God rules over the kingdom of men and appoints over it whom he will."

15. KING PEDRO II OF ARAGÓN ALLIES WITH CASTILE

But the glorious king, like a man not disheartened by adversity nor overly puffed up by prosperity,[1] manfully girded himself to defend his realm and placed his hope and trust in the power of our Lord Jesus Christ, whose faith he always believed most firmly and held and defended against every heretical depravity.[2]

At that time, Sancha, Queen of Aragón, the king of Castile's aunt, had in her care her adolescent son Pedro, King of Aragón, and his kingdom. For not long after the battle of Alarcos, Alfonso, King of Aragón, son of the count of Barcelona, the father of King Pedro, entered upon the way of all flesh.[3] Men suspected that he contrived to do whatever evil he could for the ruination of the king of Castile; but the queen loved the king of Castile more than all men, even during her husband's lifetime. For that reason, her husband hated her very much.

Now when the opportunity arose, the fire of love, which, during her husband's lifetime, had been somewhat hidden in the queen's breast, out of fear, erupted into an open flame. She closely allied her son to the king of Castile, and like a prudent Abigail,[4] strove powerfully and in every way to aid the king of Castile. But so that the king of Aragón who suffered somewhat from poverty, could more easily succor the king of Castile, he received a gift of a large sum of money from the king of Castile.[5]

On the advice of his prudent mother, King Pedro, now an adolescent, accom-

---

[1] Cf. Seneca, *De beata vita*, 4:2: "... nec extollant fortuita nec frangant. ..."

[2] The reference to heresy raises the question whether the Albigensians of southern France had found their way into the kingdom of Castile.

[3] Alfonso II of Aragón had married Sancha, a daughter of Alfonso VII of León–Castile, on 18 January 1174; thus she was Alfonso VIII's aunt. Although initially on good terms with Alfonso VIII, the king of Aragón came to resent Castilian domination; however, from August 1195 to March 1196 he made a pilgrimage to Santiago de Compostela and attempted to restore harmony among the Christian rulers. He died on 25 April 1196. His son Pedro II ruled from 1196 to 1213. See *The Chronicle of San Juan de la Peña. A Fourteenth-Century Official History of the Crown of Aragon*, trans. Lynn H. Nelson (Philadelphia: University of Pennsylvania Press, 1991), 51–56, ch. 33. The biblical locution "the way of all flesh" (cf. Psalms 65:3: "To you all flesh must come") is a favorite of our author and is repeated elsewhere (e.g., below chap. 17).

[4] 1 Samuel 25:1–43. Abigail was the wife of Nabal, and after the Lord struck him dead, she married King David.

[5] Our author regrettably does not mention the amount, but given his position in the royal court he likely knew what he was talking about.

panied by his noble vassals, came to the king of Castile and bound himself to him inseparably for as long as the war lasted. After taking wise counsel, the kings encamped in mid-summer near Ávila in a very healthy and cool place commonly called Palomera.[6] From there, if need be, they could easily support their men in Trasierra, and they defended the towns and castles against the king of Morocco and those who were in the Tierra de Campos. Thus fixed between their enemies, they caused them both to fear, because they [the enemies] could not go about as freely as they wished.

Discovering that the king of Morocco was returning to his realm,[7] they moved their forces against the king of León. They sent on ahead Fernando Rodríguez of Albarracín, a noble, prudent, and energetic man, with a host of knights to detain the king of León and his army in the kingdom of Castile so they could not return freely to their own realm.[8] But the king of León learned of this beforehand and rapidly returned to his kingdom. Though the nobleman Fernando Rodríguez could not catch him in the kingdom of Castile, he did, however, pursue him as far as his own kingdom. The kings with their army followed the knights whom they sent on ahead. They invaded the kingdom of León, ravaging the land everywhere, because there was no one to defend it. They attacked and seized by force the town of Castroverde, where Count Fernando de Cabrera, the nobleman Álvaro Pelayo, Pedro Ovárez, and Alfonso Armíldez, a certain Portuguese noble, were captured with all their knights.[9] Then advancing further, they approached Benavente where the king of León was together with Moors and his Christian vassals. They came as far as Astorga and even to Rabanal, while others pushed as far as the region called Bierzo.[10] Laying waste the surrounding regions in this manner, they returned to León and besieged the Castle of the Jews and

---

[6] Palomera or Paramera lies between Ávila and Ríofrío near the Sierra de la Paramera.

[7] The caliph retired to Seville in late August 1196 but remained there until the following spring.

[8] Fernando Rodríguez de Azagra was lord of Albarracín, a lordship lying on the frontiers between Castile and Aragón, about forty-five miles northeast of Cuenca.

[9] In July and August 1196 the kings of Castile and Aragón attacked the kingdom of León. Castroverde de Campos is about thirty-five miles west of Palencia and about thirty miles east of Benavente. In chap. 40 Pedro Ovárez appears as prior of the Hospital.

[10] Benavente lies about forty-five miles south of León; Astorga is about twenty-five miles directly west of León; Rabanal del Camino is west of Astorga; the district of Bierzo borders on Galicia.

took it by force. After fortifying it and holding it, they returned to the kingdom of Castile with great honor and much booty.[11]

In the following year, the third after the battle of Alarcos, the king of Morocco came once more to Trasierra and besieged the town called Madrid. He held it under siege for many days, but divine power protected it, through the agency of Diego López and the other nobles and people who were in the town. Giving up the siege, the king then turned against Uclés, Huete, and Cuenca, and then returned to his own realm.[12] At the same time the king of León recovered the Castle of the Jews near León. But the king of Castile and the king of Aragón again invaded the kingdom of León and did much damage to the people of León. The king of León then went to the king of Morocco whom he found at Seville.

A truce was finally arranged between the king of Morocco, who returned to Marrakech, the seat of his kingdom, and the king of Castile. Peace was also established between the king of León and the king of Castile, though it could not have been achieved otherwise, if the king of Castile had not given his daughter, Lady Berenguela, in marriage to the king of León. This was a marriage de facto, but there could be none de iure, since the two kings were related to one another in the second degree of kindred.[13]

---

[11] After a siege of four days *Castrum Iudeorum* — the Castle of the Jews — surrendered on 9 August 1196. Pedro II then returned to Aragón. Alfonso IX recovered *Castrum Iudeorum*, now Puente del Castro on the river Torío, just east of the city, and gave it to the cathedral of León on 12 July 1197: González, *Alfonso IX*, 1:87, and 2:153–154, no. 105. The Jews were sometimes allowed to garrison castles where they could enjoy autonomy and defend themselves if necessary: Yitzhak Baer, *A History of the Jews in Christian Spain*, 2 vols. (Philadelphia: Jewish Publication Society, 1966), 1:80.

[12] In April 1197 the caliph set out on another expedition against Castile, again ravaging about Talavera and Toledo, but returned to Córdoba on 15 August. Because of reports of trouble in Morocco, he agreed to a truce with Castile for five years. See Lomax, *The Reconquest of Spain*, 120–122; Kennedy, *Muslim Spain and Portugal*, 247–249.

[13] This is another instance of our author's concern with consanguinity (cf. introduction, p. xxxii). Alfonso IX and Berenguela (who was then about sixteen, and whose earlier betrothal to Conrad of Hohenstaufen had been annulled by the papal legate Cardinal Gregory) were second cousins; they were married at Valladolid in October 1197: see above, chap. 11, nn. 3, 5.

16. ALFONSO VIII AND SANCHO VII OF NAVARRE

The glorious king of Castile, not unmindful of the injuries inflicted on him and his kingdom in his time of suffering by the king of Navarre, invaded his kingdom and began to plunder it. The king of Navarre, seeing that he could not resist, left his realm and fled to the king of Morocco. He went to the city of Marrakech to implore his aid, begging him to deign to help him.[1] In the meantime, the king of Castile besieged Vitoria and during the siege seized all the surrounding castles, namely, Treviño, Arganzón, Santa Cruz, Alchorroza, Vitoria la Vieja, Arducea, the region of Guipúzcoa, and San Sebastián, Marañon, San Vicente, and some others. Vitoria surrendered to him at last, and thus he held the whole of Álava and the adjacent regions. He then returned victoriously to Castile.[2]

Bereft of all help, the king of Navarre received from the king of Morocco a certain sum of money and certain revenues assigned to him in Valencia, where he remained for a long time. According to a truce made between the king of Castile and the king of Navarre, all the castles and towns taken by the king of Castile in the kingdom of the king of Navarre remained in the power of the king of Castile.[3]

---

[1] Sancho VII personally sought help from the Muslims in Spain; he probably did not go to Marrakech, the Almohad capital in Morocco, but sent envoys instead. Cf. Rodrigo Jiménez de Rada, *Historia de rebus Hispanie*, 253–254, Bk. 7, chap. 32.

[2] The siege of Vitoria (about sixty miles northeast of Burgos) took place in the summer of 1199, and it apparently fell to Castilian arms early in 1200. The province of Álava centered around Vitoria. Alfonso VIII occupied the towns and villages south of Vitoria and north of the Ebro river: Treviño, Puebla de Arganzón, Arlucea, Santa Cruz de Campezo, Alchorroza, Marañon, and San Vicente de la Sierra. Vitoria la Vieja may be Villasuso de Vitoria. The province of Guipúzcoa lay to the northeast of Vitoria, extending to the port of San Sebastián on the Bay of Biscay.

[3] The truce was probably concluded at the beginning of 1200, but before March 1201.

17. ALFONSO VIII IN GASCONY

Following this, the glorious king of Castile, who was never at rest[1] but always active, who took no pleasure save in continual labor,[2] struggled to acquire the whole of Gascony which he believed belonged to him by right, as his father-in-law Henry, king of the English, had promised it to him. For the noble king of Castile had married King Henry's daughter, Lady Leonor, most noble in her behavior and descent, modest and very prudent. King Henry is said to have promised her, together with Gascony, to his son-in-law, the king of Castile.[3]

At that time, King John nicknamed Lackland, the brother of Queen Leonor, held the kingdom of England. King Henry had had four sons, namely, the young king, and the count of Brittany, both of whom predeceased their father; Richard, count of Poitou, who succeeded his father in the kingdom (when he returned from the lands beyond the sea he was mortally wounded by an arrow while besieging a certain castle in the land of Limousin or thereabouts, and went the way of all flesh);[4] the fourth, John Lackland, succeeded his brother Richard in the kingdom since Richard died without children.[5]

In the time of King John, whom Philip, King of the French, had deprived of Normandy, Anjou, the land of Tours, and the famous city of Poitiers,[6] the king of Castile and some of his vassals invaded Gascony, occupying almost all of it except Bayonne and Bordeaux. He also took Blaye and Bourg beyond the Garonne

---

[1] Cf. Revelation 4:8: "et requiem non habebant die ac nocte" ["day and night they do not stop exclaiming"]; Isaiah 62:6: "Never, by day or by night, shall they be silent."

[2] Cf. Ovid, *Tristia* 5.1.33: "quiesque nulla nisi in studio."

[3] In 1170 Alfonso VIII married Leonor (born in 1160), the daughter of Henry II of England and Eleanor of Aquitaine.

[4] Cf. Psalms 65:3: "To you all flesh must come." (quoted above chap. 15, n. 3).

[5] The sons of Henry II of England (1154–1189) were young Henry, who though crowned king during his father's lifetime in 1170, rebelled against him and died in 1182; Geoffrey, who married the heiress to the duchy of Brittany, and died in 1186; Richard the Lionheart, who ruled England from 1189 to 1199, participated in the Third Crusade, and died in a petty quarrel with one of his vassals; and John, nicknamed Lackland because he had not been assigned any lands when Henry II apportioned his dominions among his sons in 1169, who succeeded Richard as king of England and ruled until 1216.

[6] Philip II Augustus, king of France (1180–1223), declared King John a contumacious vassal in 1202 and dispossessed him of Normandy and the other fiefs that the kings of England held of the French crown. See Elizabeth M. Hallam, *Capetian France, 987–1328* (London and New York: Longman, 1980), 182–183.

and the land between the two seas [Entre-deux-Mers] and then returned to his kingdom.

Before he went to Gascony he had made a truce with the king of León. On returning from Gascony he confirmed the peace with that king and received Lord Diego López whom he had previously exiled for a long time.[7]

The reason for the discord between the glorious king of Castile and the king of León was this: the king of León had put away the queen, Lady Berenguela, the king of Castile's daughter. The king of León already had two sons and two daughters by her.[8]

The noble king of Castile, therefore, a wise and discreet man, realized that to strive for the acquisition of Gascony was to plow the seashore;[9] but driven by a certain necessity, once having begun, he could not desist. The poverty of the land and the inconstancy of men in whom one rarely found fidelity made the land of Gascony hateful to the king, but love of his wife compelled him to persist pertinaciously in his undertaking lest she be disappointed. But at last, seeing that he could not succeed, he absolved the Gascons, both the nobles and the people of the cities, from the oath and homage by which they were bound to him.

This was a happy day,[10] always loved[11] in the kingdom of Castile, when the king yielded to persistence and desisted from this undertaking! Gascony would have wasted the inexhaustible source of gold and would have exhausted the nobility of the magnates.[12]

---

[7] Alfonso VIII's acquisition of Álava and Guipúzcoa in 1199 from the king of Navarre was one of the reasons for the discord between him and Diego López de Haro, lord of Vizcaya.

[8] The papal legate had excommunicated Alfonso IX and Berenguela not long after their marriage in 1197. Despite papal insistence, they did not separate until the spring of 1204. Meanwhile, Berenguela gave birth to a daughter, Leonor, in 1198, and to a son, the future Fernando III, in 1201. Two other children were born before they separated. See Joseph F. O'Callaghan, "Innocent III and the Kingdoms of Castile and León," in *Pope Innocent III and his World*, ed. John C. Moore (Aldershot: Ashgate, 1999), 317–335.

[9] Cf. Virgil, *Aeneid* 4.212: "*litus arandum*" (our Latin text has *litus arare*).

[10] 1 Maccabees 10:55: "Happy the day on which you returned to the land of your fathers and took your seat upon the royal throne!"

[11] Horace, *Carmina* 1.5.10: "*semper amabilem.*"

[12] Alfonso VIII invaded Gascony in the summer of 1205 and probably again in the summer of 1206. Our author clearly condemns the expenditure of money on the conquest of Gascony. See González, *Alfonso VIII*, 1:864–875.

18. INFANTE FERNANDO AND THE WAR WITH THE MOORS

Before the noble king invaded Gascony he gave his daughter, a girl named Blanca (who is now crowned queen of the French), in marriage to Louis, son of Philip, King of the French; he now reigns in the kingdom of France in his father's place.[1] After he returned from Gascony he gave his other daughter, Urraca, as a bride to Afonso, the son of Sancho, king of Portugal; he reigned in that kingdom after his father Sancho.[2]

At the same time the glorious king had two sons, Fernando and Enrique. When Fernando reached the age of puberty, he was so very generous (I will not say prodigal), that even when he gave much, he thought that he had given nothing, if there were still more begging, whose cupidity he was not sufficiently able to satisfy. Nobles from every part of Spain, all of whom he received like closest acquaintances and whose indigence he relieved with many gifts, flocked to him in droves. The beardless youth, escaping at last from his guardian, rejoiced in horses and dogs and in the grass of sunny fields.[3] He played with different kinds of birds. His manners were praised above measure by his equals.

When he was a little older, around the end of adolescence, he clothed himself with prudence and, with the strength of his young age, began to disdain all the aforesaid things in which he had gloried, and began to attend to the use of arms, willingly clinging to those whom he knew to be vigorous in arms and expert in military affairs. He burned with a desire for war with the Saracens. Discussing it with his friends and often turning it over in his mind, no other study could now please him except knighthood and the use of arms.[4]

The glorious king, seeing his son's desire and his beauty (for he was exceedingly handsome) and the strength of his youthful age, was pleased with him, and gave thanks to the Lord who had given him such a son, who could now be his helper

---

[1] On 23 May 1200 Blanca, or Blanche, was married to Philip Augustus's son, Louis VIII (1223–1226), the future king of France. Blanche later acted as regent for their son Louis IX (1226–1270), who was later canonized as a saint. She died in 1253 while he was on the Sixth Crusade. The language here indicates that this part of the *Chronicle* was written between 1223 and 1226.

[2] In 1208 Urraca was married to Afonso II (1211–1223), the son of Sancho I of Portugal.

[3] A quotation of Horace, *Ars Poetica*, 161–162: "Imberbis iuuenis, tandem custode remoto, / gaudet equis canibusque et aprici gramine campi."

[4] One wonders whether the author had some responsibility for the education of Infante Fernando, who now turned away from books to knightly pursuits.

in the government of the kingdom, and could in part take his place in warlike affairs. The misfortune which he had suffered in the battle of Alarcos remained fixed deep in the king's mind;[5] he had never erased it. Oftentimes he recalled that day to mind, desiring to have revenge on the king of Morocco, and for this he often prayed to the Lord.

The Most High, who is a patient accountant,[6] seeing the desire of the glorious king, inclined His ear and from the seat of His glory on high heard his prayer.[7] The spirit of the Lord came upon the glorious king[8] and strength from on high clothed him,[9] so that what he had previously thought about for a long time, he brought about in action. Therefore, confiding in the mercy of our Lord Jesus Christ, he went to war against the king of Morocco, and with his son, entered at once into the land of that king, toward the region of Murcia. But since he had few vassals he could not inflict much damage on the Moors.[10] But while he operated in that area, his vassals Alfonso Téllez and Rodrigo Rodríguez, with certain people from Toledo, besieged the tower of Guadalerzas and, after using machines against it, took it by force.[11]

Now when the king of Morocco, the fourth from 'Abd al-Mu'min, the son of the one who came to Alarcos,[12] heard that the king of Castile had gone to war

---

[5] Virgil, *Aeneid* 1.26: "manet alta mente repostum" (here incorrectly positum, quoted above, chap. 14, n. 2).

[6] Sirach 5:4: "For the Lord bides his time."

[7] Cf. Psalms 3:5: "When I call out to the Lord, he answers me from his holy mountain."

[8] Cf. Judges 14:6: "But the spirit of the Lord came upon Samson."

[9] Cf. e.g., Luke 24:49: "Stay in the city until you are clothed with power from on high."

[10] The truce with the Almohads expired in 1210. Alfonso VIII made an incursion into the kingdom of Murcia in May 1211.

[11] Alfonso Téllez de Meneses and Rodrigo Rodríguez captured Guadalerzas, in the modern province of Ciudad Real about forty miles south of Toledo; it had been lost in 1195 after the battle of Alarcos.

[12] The Latin text reads: "Rex uero Marroquitanus quartus Abdelimum, filius eius, qui uenit ad Alarcos. . . ." Charlo Brea translated that as "El rey marroquí Abdelmon IV, hijo del que vino a Alarcos. . . ." Cirot noted that the preposition *ab* should follow *quartus*, meaning "the fourth from", but he also indicated that the text should have read *tercius*, "the third from 'Abd al-Mu'min." That interpretation is borne out by the succession of the caliphs: 'Abd al-Mu'min (d. 1163), Abû Ya'qûb Yûsuf (d. 1184); Ya'qûb al-Mansûr (d. 1199), and Muhammad al-Nasir (d. 1214). Muhammad would thus be the third caliph from 'Abd al-Mu'min. In addition Muhammad did not bear the name 'Abd al-Mu'min, as

against him, he was full of indignation and fury. Like a vigorous and warlike man, impatient of delay, he gathered a vast host of knights and foot soldiers, and opened his treasures[13] to distribute most generous stipends to his men,[14] for the kingdom of Morocco then flourished in prudence and riches. And with a multitude of warriors he crossed over [the Strait of Gibraltar].[15]

He made the journey through Seville and Córdoba, passing through the Puerto del Muradal, and besieged the castle called Salvatierra, then the seat of the Knighthood of the friars of Calatrava. It was fortified with many different kinds of arms, with grain and barley and many kinds of vegetables, meats, and vigorous men, the friars, namely, and other nobles and distinguished men. The siege was established and with machines of awesome size they began to assault the castle, which otherwise seemed impregnable.[16]

Charlo Brea's reading would have it, and the usage of the numeral IV would be totally foreign to the author of the *Latin Chronicle*.

[13] Matthew 2:11: "Then they opened their treasures. . . ."

[14] The kings of Castile and León ordinarily maintained their vassals by means of stipends (*stipendia, solidata, soldadas*), rather then fiefs as was customary in France.

[15] The Almohad caliph, Muhammad ibn Ya'qûb, known by his honorific name, an-Nasir (1199–1213), or more commonly to the Christians as Miramamolín, crossed the Strait in May 1211; he left Seville on 15 June.

[16] After the battle of Alarcos in 1195 the Almohads had captured Calatrava and other fortresses belonging to the Order of that name. Sometime between 1196 and 1198 the knights occupied Salvatierra, a fortress situated about twenty miles south of Ciudad Real and directly opposite the castle known later as Calatrava la Nueva. For about thirteen years the knights were known as the Order of Salvatierra. The siege was begun in late June or early July. The Puerto del Muradal, now known as Despeñaperros, was a pass through the mountains, just to the south of Salvatierra. See O'Callaghan, "The Order of Calatrava, 1158–1212," 422–425; and cf. above, chap. 12, n. 6.

19. THE FALL OF SALVATIERRA, SEPTEMBER 1211

On hearing this, the noble king ordered Lord Diego to remain at Toledo together with his vassals and certain other magnates. Now the king himself went about through the towns and castles in Trasierra, comforting the minds of men; but the army which he was able to assemble remained in the Sierra of San Vicente, because few of the towns joined him at that time.[1]

After two months and longer, at the command of the glorious king, the castle of Salvatierra surrendered to the king of Morocco, because they were no longer able to defend it. The lives of those who were within were spared and the movable goods that they could carry with them were saved. O what great mourning among men, the cry of women moaning and striking their breasts[2] for the loss of Salvatierra![3]

But through the mercy and power of our Lord Jesus Christ, who is the helper of His people in good times and in tribulation,[4] that mourning was turned into joy[5] within a year.

With a certain presentiment that castle was truly indeed called Salvatierra because, by means of that castle, the Lord doubly saved the whole land, for the invasion of the king of Morocco, which could have resulted in many injuries, harmed the realm not at all during that year. The capture of Salvatierra, moreover, was the special occasion of the glorious battle that occurred in the following year at Las Navas de Tolosa, in which through the power of the cross of Christ the king of Morocco was conquered.

For the glorious king, touched inwardly with sorrow in his heart,[6] placed his

---

[1] The Sierra de San Vicente is near Talavera, to the west of Toledo, along the Tagus river.

[2] Cf. Matthew 2:18 (Jeremiah 31:15: "In Ramah is heard the sound of moaning, of bitter weeping!"); Luke 23:27: "A large crowd of people followed Jesus, including many women who mourned and lamented him."

[3] Salvatierra surrrendered in September 1211 after a siege of fifty-one days. The caliph proclaimed his triumph to the Muslim world in a letter dated 13 September at Andújar. See Lomax, *The Reconquest of Spain,* 122–123; Kennedy, *Muslim Spain and Portugal,* 249–254.

[4] Psalms 9:10. "The Lord is a stronghold for the oppressed, a stronghold in times of distress." The Latin here is not that of the Vulgate, but that of the Septuagint.

[5] Esther C:10 (13:17): "turn our sorrow into joy."

[6] Genesis 6:6: "When the Lord saw how great was man's wickedness on earth . . . his heart was grieved" (quoted above, chap. 4, n. 1 and chap. 12, n. 5).

soul in His hands,[7] took counsel and deliberation with his son and with Lord Diego and the archbishop of Toledo and the other magnates of the kingdom; putting their hope in God,[8] it was decided that in the next year they would fight against the king of Morocco, if he did not challenge him. Therefore an edict went forth from the glorious king through the whole realm, that the construction of walls on which all were laboring should be interrupted and all should appear with arms of war and prepare themselves for the future battle.[9]

---

[7] Cf. Luke 23:46: "Father, into your hands I commend my spirit."

[8] Psalms 78:7: "that they too might put their trust in God."

[9] The date of the edict can be calculated from the date of the death of Infante Fernando mentioned in chap. 20. The edict was dated on Michaelmas, the feast of St. Michael, 29 September 1211, about two weeks before the Infante died.

20. THE DEATH OF INFANTE FERNANDO

After this, before fifteen days had scarcely passed, the king's son, Fernando, the flower of young men, the adornment of the kingdom, the right hand of his father, was seized with an acute fever and gave up his life at Madrid.[1] The king's heart broke; his princes and the nobles of the realm were stunned; the people of the cities were wasted away. Wise men were terrified,[2] noting that the wrath and indignation of God had decreed that the land should be desolate.[3] Mourning was everywhere. The aged sprinkled their heads with ashes; everyone put on sackcloth and ashes; all the virgins dressed in mourning;[4] the face of the land was changed deeply.[5]

The most noble queen Leonor, hearing of her son's death, wanted to die with him and got into the bed on which her son lay; placing her mouth to his mouth and clasping his hand in her hand,[6] she tried either to revive him or to die with him. Those who saw it said that never was seen sorrow like unto hers.[7] With the people, let us cry out: "O the height of the riches of the wisdom and knowledge of God! How incomprehensible are His judgments and uncertain His ways!"[8]

---

[1] Infante Fernando, born on 29 November 1189, died at the age of 21 on 14 October 1211.

[2] Jeremiah 8:9: "The wise are confounded, dismayed and ensnared."

[3] Jeremiah 12:11: "They have made it a mournful waste, desolate it lies before me."

[4] In his first edition of the *Crónica*, 25, Charlo Brea read "omnes virgines scalide translating it as desfallecieron" ["all the virgins swooned"]. In the second edition of the *Chronica*, 55, he read: "omnes virgines squalide," and in his second translation, *Crónica*, 47, translated it as "all the virgins fasted." "Dressed in mourning" seems a better rendering of squalide. This is a quotation from Lamentations 1:4: "Virgines eius squalidae"; *NAB* reads: "Her virgins sigh." Douay: "her virgins are in affliction."

[5] Jonah 3:6–8: "When the news reached the king of Nineveh, he rose from his throne, laid aside his robe, covered himself with sackcloth, and sat in the ashes. Then he had this proclaimed throughout Nineveh ... 'Man and beast shall be covered with sackcloth and call loudly to God.'"; Lamentations 2:10: "They strew dust on their heads and gird themselves with sackcloth; the maidens of Jerusalem bow their heads to the ground."

[6] 2 Kings 4:34: "Then he [Elisha] lay upon the child on the bed, placing his mouth upon the child's mouth, his eyes upon the eyes, and his hands upon the hands."

[7] Lamentations 1:12: "See whether there is any suffering like my suffering."

[8] Romans 11 33: "Oh, the depth of the riches and wisdom and knowledge of God! How inscrutable are his judgments and how unsearchable his ways."

How very deep are his thoughts! and we foolish ones do not understand.[9]

What seemed to be the beginning of woe and the confirmation of evil was the end of evil and the beginning of joy and consolation. Now the king's son was buried in the royal monastery located near Burgos, by the hand of the archbishop of Toledo in the presence of Queen Lady Berenguela and amidst all the lamentations of everyone in Castile. But the glorious king and his wife and Lord Diego remained in Trasierra. The archbishop and Queen Lady Berenguela returned to the king whom they found at Guadalajara.[10]

Then Rodrigo, archbishop of Toledo, was sent to the king of France and to the princes and other nobles of those parts to make known to them the distress of the Christian people and the danger of the war to come. The noble king went to Cuenca where he had an interview with his friend King Pedro of Aragón, and bound him to him by oath that, on the eighth day of the feast of Pentecost next, he would be at Toledo with the king of Castile, ready for war against the king of Morocco.

At the end of the interview, each went his separate way. The noble king, endowed with strength from on high,[11] went to the castle called Alarcón. Then, having sent his wife and daughter away, with a few knights and men from some of the towns and from his household, within fifteen days he captured the noble castle of Jorquera which seemed impregnable, and the castle of Alcalá and Las Cuevas de Garandén, all of which he fortified with arms and men; thus with joy he returned to his land.[12]

---

[9] Psalms 92:6–7: "How profound your purpose! A senseless person cannot know this; a fool cannot understand." From the text it does not appear that our author was an eyewitness to the queen's sorrow.

[10] The burial, presided over by Archbishop Rodrigo of Toledo, took place in the Cistercian nunnery of Las Huelgas, on the outskirts of Burgos, founded by the king and queen in 1187. Queen Berenguela, the former wife of Alfonso IX of León, was Infante Fernando's sister.

[11] Again cf. Luke 24:49: "Stay in the city until you are clothed with power from on high."

[12] Jorquera, Alcalá del Júcar, and Las Cuevas de Garandén lie on the river Júcar, about forty miles southeast of Alarcón, which is about thirty miles southeast of Cuenca; the king had returned to Alarcón by 29 November.

21. GATHERING OF CRUSADERS IN TOLEDO

This was the beginning of joy. All those who had lost heart, from sorrow and anxiety because of the capture of Salvatierra and the death of the king's son, were comforted in the Lord and in the power of His goodness, so much so that from then on the greatest desire of everyone, both nobles and non-nobles, was to lash out at the king of Morocco in battle. Indeed, the power of our Lord Jesus Christ, who is truly God and man, worked quietly so that He could suddenly change the hearts of men from fear to boldness, from despair to the highest confidence.

The archbishop of Toledo went to the king of France, to whom he explained the reason for his journey and the need and the distress of the Christian people; but he could not get a good word from his mouth. He traveled through the whole of France, begging the magnates and promising them many things in the name of the king of Castile, but neither could he rouse any of them.[1] Moreover, the noble king, who had put his whole intent and determination into this, sent his physician, Master Arnald, a diligent man, to arouse the minds of the powerful in the region of Poitou and Gascony; he promised many things in the king's name for the future war.

From those regions many nobles and magnates, together with the archbishop of Bordeaux, came to the aid of the king of Castile in the following summer when the time for war was already imminent. Also from the region of Provence through which the archbishop had passed there came the archbishop of Narbonne and certain others from the province of Vienne.[2]

Around the feast of Pentecost, therefore, men began to come together from everywhere to the city of Toledo, and on the eighth day of the same feast, Pedro, the king of Aragón, entered Toledo as he had promised, accompanied by only one knight. Later many of his good vassals, expert in military affairs, followed him.[3]

While the nobles and people of the kings of Castile and Aragón assembled, the noble king of Castile provided sufficiently for all the expenses of everyone who had come from Poitou, Gascony, and Provence, and from other regions, and of the king of Aragón himself. Such a quantity of gold was distributed there every day that the counters and the weighers could scarcely reckon the multitude of

---

[1] Philip Augustus, king of France, was preoccupied with his own struggle against King John of England.

[2] William Amanieu was archbishop of Bordeaux. The archbishop of Narbonne, Arnald Amaury, entered Toledo on 3 June 1212.

[3] Pentecost fell on Sunday, 13 May; the octave was 20 May.

coins necessary for expenses. At the king's request, all the clergy of the kingdom of Castile had granted one-half of all their revenues that year to the lord king.

Besides the daily stipend to the king of Aragón, he sent a large sum of money to him before he left his kingdom because he was poor and obligated by many debts; without the help of the king of Castile he could not have supplied the necessary stipends to the knights who were obliged to follow him.

Thus, enflamed by a desire for the coming conflict, they all hastened to decamp, but the Poitevins and others from beyond the mountains did not have horses suitable for war nor beasts of burden to carry the baggage needed for the expedition. The noble soul of the glorious prince, who showered gold like water, gave generously to all of them what they needed.

22. THE ADVANCE TO THE PUERTO DEL MURADAL

Breaking camp, therefore, in the name of the Lord Jesus Christ, they advanced toward Malagón; in a moment, as if in the wink of an eye, they ripped it from the hands of the Moors and cut to pieces[1] as many people as they found there. Then as they approached Calatrava, it was surrendered to them by the hand of the Moor called Ibn Qalam; the lives of the men and women who were found there were saved. They then took Benavente, Alarcos, and Caracuel.[2]

But the ultramontanes who were accustomed to live in the shadows of temperate regions, considering the excess of the summer and the heat of the sun, began to complain, saying that they had come to fight the king of Morocco, as had been preached to them; but as they had not encountered him, they wanted in every way to return home. All the Christians who heard this were saddened as they prepared to withdraw. For there were almost 1,000 noble knights, vigorous and powerful in arms, and almost 60,000 armed foot soldiers, of whom the archbishop of Bordeaux was in effect the head and leader.[3]

The noble king and the king of Aragón tried to restrain them, but they could not achieve this in any way. Although the noble king was advised to frighten them with harsh words and threats, because they had consumed his goods and had received many gifts from him, he did not, however, acquiesce in that advice, but allowed them to depart in peace; he gave gifts and expenses to the archbishop of Bordeaux. But then the army of the king of Morocco was only two days' journey away from the Christian army.

Awesome in His saints is God,[4] who so marvelously granted to Spain and

---

[1] Charlo Brea reads concidentes in frustra and translates it matando inútilmente; but Cirot suggests concidentes in frusta, that is, mettant en pièces, or cutting to pieces. This is not in Charlo Brea's apparatus.

[2] The army left Toledo on 20 June; Malagón, about twenty miles north of Ciudad Real, was taken on 24 June. Calatrava la vieja (about twenty miles southeast) capitulated on 1 July. Alarcos (about nine miles west), Benavente (about ten miles west), Caracuel (about twenty miles southwest), and Piedrabuena (about twenty miles west of Ciudad Real) were taken on 5–6 July.

[3] The ultramontanes (the French) withdrew on 3 July. The numbers of knights and foot soldiers are obviously exaggerated.

[4] "Mirabilis Deus in sanctis suis;" Cabanes Pecourt (following the London MS) reads "in factis suis" ["in his deeds"]; Psalms 67:36, following the Septuagint, has "mirabilis . . . sanctis"; Psalms 68(67):36: "Awesome is God in his holy place" translates the Vulgate "terribilis . . . de sanctuario."

especially to the kingdom of Castile that, on the withdrawal of the ultramontanes, the glory of the victory in the famous battle should be attributed to the Spaniards, and not to the ultramontanes. But while they departed, a few remained with Theobald of Blazón, the son of Pedro Rodríguez de Guzmán, and with the archbishop of Narbonne who had been born in Catalonia.

Now the Christians, roused out of the thoughts that at first had saddened them, moved their army toward Salvatierra, where they encamped. But on the next day they remained there, and, on the order of the king, both nobles and people armed and marched out into the field as though they were ready to fight the enemy. Terrifying indeed were the ordered ranks of the camp.[5] Never had so many and such kinds of iron weapons been seen in the Spains. Stirred by such a pleasing and terrifying sight, the kings were greatly encouraged. The expected hope of victory added strength to the minds and bodies of everyone.[6]

The army was moved quickly and cheerfully toward the Puerto del Muradal. As they were approaching it, they discovered for certain that part of the army of the king of Morocco held the Puerto de Losa through which no one was allowed to pass without their consent.

The magnates met together. The king of Aragón and the king of Navarre (who was then already present, although he had come with a few knights), the archbishops of Toledo and Narbonne, Diego López, the noble vassal of the glorious king, and other magnates of both kingdoms, assembled in the tent of the king of Castile to deliberate about what should be done in such great necessity. To some it seemed that each should return to his own land, because he could do so with honor and glory, for in no way was it possible to cross the mountains. But to others it seemed that they should look for another pass. But it seemed to the glorious king to be dishonorable to retrace his steps. At the hour of vespers they separated, without having discovered any counsel that pleased them; but they decided to implore divine aid according to the advice of King Josaphat of whom one reads in the book of Kings, "when we do not know what we ought to do, we have this alone remaining: that we lift up our eyes to heaven."[7]

---

[5] Song of Songs 6:4: "as awe-inspiring as bannered troops."

[6] This review of the Christian army took place on 8 July.

[7] Cf. 2 Chronicles 20:12: "We are at a loss what to do, hence our eyes are turned toward you."

THE REIGN OF ALFONSO VIII

23. A SHEPHERD REVEALS A PASSAGE
THROUGH THE MOUNTAINS

Only García Romero, a noble man, a prudent, strong, and faithful vassal of the king of Aragón, remained with the glorious king in his tent. Then God sent a certain person in the guise of a shepherd who spoke secretly to the glorious king, promising to show, to whomever he should designate, a place quite nearby through which the whole army could cross the highest mountains without danger.[1]

Elated with great joy, the king ordered García Romero to approach and told him what the shepherd had said. Immediately, on the order of the glorious king, he went out and summoned his knights; when the sun was already setting, with the shepherd leading him, he came to a certain place where he saw with his eyes what the shepherd had promised to the noble king. Rejoicing and clapping his hands, he returned quickly to the glorious king and informed him that he had found it to be just as the shepherd had said.

It was believed by those who know rightly that that was not an ordinary man but some divine power which came to the aid of the Christian people in such difficulty, because even though so many military commanders, so many shepherds, so many friars of Calatrava had often crossed through those places, none of them knew anything about that place; nor did the shepherd appear afterward.

They were silent that night. On the break of day, that news was spread through the camps. All were filled with great joy. Breaking camp, that same day, a Saturday,[2] they passed through steep slopes and deep valleys. Descending onto a plain, they encamped opposite the camp of the king of Morocco. When the Moors saw the Christian camp, they were filled both with wonder and with fear.

On the following morning, Sunday,[3] the Moors marched out onto the field prepared to fight, but the Christians rested that day, defending the tents from the attack of the Saracens. The Moors, puffed up with pride, dashed round about impetuously, almost reaching the Christian tents; but realizing that the Christians did not wish to fight that day, they returned as victors to their camp site with their king.

The dawn of the sun shone brightly[4] announcing the most brilliant and most

---

[1] This was the night of 12–13 July.

[2] 14 July 1212.

[3] 15 July 1212.

[4] This is the beginning of an ancient Easter hymn, *Aurora solis rutilat,* or *Aurora lucis rutilat;* some verses were included in the hymn for Lauds.

felicitous day; if the glorious king and his kingdom had incurred any blemish or disgrace in the battle of Alarcos, it was going to be erased that day by the power of Our Lord Jesus Christ and of the most victorious cross, which the king of Morocco had blasphemed with a foul mouth. When he heard that the glorious king had sent the archbishop of Toledo and his legates to France and to other Christian regions to invite people adhering to the Catholic faith to come to the battle, the king of Morocco was reported to have said that he was strong enough to fight against all who adored the sign of the cross.

O Lord, Jesus Christ, you have cast him down while he was exalted;[5] for such ones are raised up on high by unrestrained pride, so that they may fall down more quickly.[6]

---

[5] Psalms 73:18: "You have hurled them down while they were raised up," following the Septuagint, not the Vulgate.

[6] Cf. Matthew 23:12: "Whoever exalts himself will be humbled; but whoever humbles himself will be exalted." Charlo Brea noted that this is an exact quotation of Claudian, *In Rufinum,* 1:22–23.

24. The Battle of Las Navas de Tolosa, 16 July 1212[1]

Then the Christians arose after midnight, the hour at which Christ, whom they worshipped, rose up victorious over death. After hearing the solemnities of masses, and being renewed by the life-giving sacrament of the Body and Blood of Jesus Christ, our God, they fortified themselves with the sign of the cross. They quickly took up their weapons of war, and with joy rushed to the battle as if they were invited to a feast. Neither the broken and stony places, nor the hollows of the valleys nor the steep mountains held them back. They advanced on the enemy prepared to die or to conquer.[2]

In the first rank at the side of the glorious king was his noble, faithful, and powerful vassal Diego López, and with him, Sancho Fernández, son of Fernando, king of León and his sister [Diego López's] Urraca;[3] his son, Lope Díaz, and his other relatives, friends and vassals. At the side of the king of Aragón, García Romero, a noble, energetic, and faithful man, commanded the first rank; with him were many other noble and powerful Aragonese. Now the other ranks were arranged on the right and the left as the order of battle requires. The kings commanded the last ranks, each separately from the other. For his part the king of Navarre had a line nobly prepared with arms and men, so that whoever passed before his sight [. . .] would not return even if they walked.[4]

---

[1] Las Navas de Tolosa was located about twenty miles northwest of Úbeda. For a detailed description of the battle see Huici Miranda, *Las grandes batallas de la reconquista,* 219–330.

[2] Compare St. Bernard of Clairvaux, *Liber de laude novae militiae,* chap. 1, PL 182:922: "Rejoice, brave warrior, if you live and you conquer in the Lord, but rejoice the more if you die and you join the Lord . . . for if they are blessed who die in the Lord (Revelation 14:13), how much more so are they who die for the Lord."

[3] Fernando II had a liaison with Urraca López de Haro, by whom he had several children, one of whom was Sancho Fernández; after the death of his first wife, Teresa of Portugal, the king married Urraca around 1187. She was the sister of Diego López de Haro, lord of Vizcaya. His son was Lope Díaz.

[4] There is a lacuna in the *Chronica* following "before his sight." In his first translation of the *Crónica,* 33, Charlo Brea omitted the lacuna and read the passage: "así todos los que delante de él pasaban no volvían aunque caminaran." In his second translation, *Crónica,* 53, he marked the lacuna and quoted the passage from Ezekiel 1:14 in the Spanish version of the Jerusalem Bible: "cada cual marchaba de frente . . . y no se volvían a caminar." In his 1997 apparatus he cites Ezekiel 1:12: "Each went straight forward; wherever the spirit wished to go, there they went; they did not turn when they moved." Cf. 1:17: "They

Those lined up in the first ranks discovered that the Moors were ready for battle. They attacked, fighting against one another, hand-to-hand, with lances, swords, and battle-axes; there was no room for archers. The Christians pressed on; the Moors repelled them; the clashing and tumult of arms was heard. The battle was joined, but neither side was overcome, although at times they pushed back the enemy, and at other times they were driven back by the enemy.

At one point certain wretched Christians who were retreating and fleeing cried out that the Christians were overcome. When the glorious and noble king of Castile, who was prepared rather to die than to be conquered,[5] heard that cry of doom, he ordered the man who carried his standard before him, to spur his horse and hasten quickly up the hill where the force of the battle was; he did so at once. When the Christians came up, the Moors thought that new waves had come upon them and fell back, overcome by the power of our Lord Jesus Christ.

The king of Morocco, who was sitting in the midst of his men surrounded by warriors chosen for battle, got up and mounted a horse or a mare, and turned tail and fled. His men were killed and slaughtered in droves, and the site of the camp and the tents of the Moors became the tombs of the fallen. Those who escaped from the battle wandered scattered about the mountains like sheep without a shepherd;[6] wherever they were found, they were slaughtered.[7]

could move in any of the four directions they faced, without veering as they moved." This comparison is with Ezekiel's visionary creatures.

[5] See below, chap. 25, n. 4.

[6] Mark 6:34: "for they were like sheep without a shepherd."

[7] See O'Callaghan, *Medieval Spain*, 245–249; Lomax, *The Reconquest of Spain*, 124–128; Kennedy, *Muslim Spain and Portugal*, 255–256.

25. THE ADVANCE TO ÚBEDA AND BAEZA

Who can count how many thousands of Moors fell that day and descended into the depths of hell? On the Christian side very few were killed that day. The Christians could sing with the psalmist: "Lord, Lord, my God, who trains my hands for battle and my fingers for war; my mercy and my refuge, my defender and my deliverer," et cetera.[1]

Satiated with the spilling of Moorish blood, and tired by the weight of arms and the heat and great thirst, the Christians, as evening was already falling, returned to the Moorish camp and rested there that night; there they found an abundance of food which they needed. Then breaking camp, they advanced farther on; discovering that the noble castle of Vilches was evacuated and abandoned, they entered and fortified it. They also seized Baños and Tolosa and Ferral. Then they went on and besieged Úbeda, where they found a countless multitude of Moors shut up inside.[2]

Deserting other cities such as Baeza, which they found to be empty,[3] and other neighboring towns, they [the Moors] had all flooded into Úbeda, a stronger place and more suitable for their defense. But that throng shut up inside was heavy and burdensome to themselves and because of great crowding, they almost died.

The Moors saw the power of the Christians, who were already prevailing against them, vigorously attacking them; they also understood that they lacked any counsel and aid because the king of Morocco had fled to Seville and was preparing to cross [the Strait of Gibraltar]. They delivered themselves into the hands of the glorious king and the king of Aragón, under such an agreement that, although their lives were saved, they and all their goods would become booty for their enemies. As reported by some of the Moors themselves who were then captured in the town and were believed to know the number of those within, almost 100,000 Saracens, including children and women, were captured there. All the movable goods and precious objects found there were given to the king of Aragón

---

[1] Psalms 144(143):1–2: "Blessed be the Lord, my rock, who trains my hands for battle, my fingers for war; My refuge and my fortress, my stronghold, my deliverer, my shield in whom I trust, who subdues peoples under me." The number of Moors killed is, of course, a great exaggeration, as is the notion that only a few Christians fell.

[2] 18 July. The castles of Vilches, Baños de la Encina, Tolosa, and Ferral were all situated within a few miles of Las Navas de Tolosa.

[3] The crusaders entered Baeza on 20 July.

and to those who had come with him to the battle. He also took many Moors with him as captives. That cursed multitude, which was shut up in the town, was dispersed and distributed through all the lands of the Christians, although so few from different parts of the world took part in that glorious and triumphant battle.[4]

They proposed to move on farther, but God, whose will no one can resist,[5] seemed to prevent it. For the judgments of God are hidden.[6] Perhaps the Christians were somewhat elated and full of pride on account of the victory in that battle, which they ought to have attributed to God alone and not to themselves.[7] Now when they had stayed for a few days in the siege of that town, a multiple variety of illnesses, and especially flux of the stomach [diarrhea], afflicted so many Christians that there were few healthy ones, who, if need be, could defend them against the enemy. Also at that time there was such great mortality among those who had remained apart from the battle that in the autumn a great number of the elderly and the aged in the towns and cities reached the end of life.

Therefore, seeing that there was no way that they could advance farther, the kings took counsel and diligent deliberation. It seemed to almost everyone that they should return to their land. So they broke down part of the wall of the town and burned the houses, and chopped down the trees and vines that they could cut down; they also left Baeza in desolation. They fortified the castles mentioned above with men, arms, and other necessities, and returned home with victory, honor, and much booty.

Then the glorious king restored to the king of Navarre, who had come to his aid, although with a few men, certain of those castles that the noble king had seized in the kingdom of Navarre. After conquering and overthrowing a very proud enemy, the glorious and noble king was received in Toledo with exultation and joy by all the people, who cried out saying: "Blessed is he who comes in the name of the Lord."[8]

---

[4] Úbeda was under siege from 20 to 23 July. The number of captives is greatly exaggerated.

[5] Cf. Job 9:13–15: "God, whose wrath no man can resist" (Douay).

[6] Cf. Psalms 36:7: "Your justice is like the highest mountains, your judgments like the mighty deep."

[7] Psalms 113B:1: "Not to us, O Lord, not to us, but to thy name give glory" (Douay).

[8] Psalms 118(117):26: "Blessed is he who comes in the name of the Lord"; Luke 19:38: "Blessed is the king who comes in the name of the Lord" (the Palm Sunday acclamation repeated at the end of the Sanctus in the Mass). Alfonso VIII probably returned to Toledo by early August.

At the time of this noble triumph, when the Catholic kings and their vassals risked their lives and kingdoms for the exaltation of the Christian name, the king of León waged war against the king of Castile, as he had done at the time of the other battle [of Alarcos]. The glorious king, wishing to end his life with honor and glory in the war against the Moors, did not call to mind what the king of León had done, but wanted to settle amicably with him so that they could help one another against the Moors.

26. THE CAPTURE OF ALCÁNTARA AND
THE SIEGE OF BAEZA

In the meantime, while peace was being discussed, around the beginning of Lent following the battle, the glorious king, whose entire purpose it was, took with him a few knights, his household guards, and certain of the townsmen from Trasierra, and went to the castle of Dueñas, which is now called Calatrava la Nueva; he took it and kept it.[1] Then he took Eznavexore, a place now called Santiago; it is a castle of the friars of the Knighthood of Santiago near Montiel.[2]

Then with the few men who were with him he besieged the noble castle of Alcaraz, which was something to be wondered at. However, after Lord Diego and certain other magnates came up the siege was strengthened. The [castle] was attacked forcefully and powerfully with marvelous machines. At length, by the grace of God, it surrendered to the glorious king, saving the lives of the Moors who were there at that time. On the feast of the Ascension, after purging the filthiness of the Moors who abandoned the town, the glorious king was received in the town with a solemn procession by the archbishop of Toledo; on the same day the archbishop celebrated mass there.[3]

Next the noble king captured another castle strongly fortified by nature, called Riopar, between Segura and Alcaraz. Then with honor and glory he returned to the area of Guadalajara around the feast of Pentecost.[4]

From there he set out on his journey to the land of Castile. His sole and great desire was to end his last days against the Saracens for the exaltation of the name of Jesus Christ; but he saw that the king of León presented a great impediment to such a holy and laudable purpose. Giving many stipends to the nobles and great

---

[1] Dueñas, about twenty miles south of Ciudad Real, lies just southwest of the castle of Salvatierra; it was taken in February 1213 though Salvatierra remained in Muslim hands until 1226. The king restored Dueñas to the Order of Calatrava, which transferred its headquarters there by 1221 and renamed it Calatrava la nueva. See O'Callaghan, "The Order of Calatrava: Years of Crisis and Survival," 425–427.

[2] Exnavexore, renamed Castellar de Santiago, is situated about seventy miles southeast of Ciudad Real and twenty miles southeast of Valdepeñas; it was taken in March 1213 and given to the Military Order of Santiago, which controlled an extensive lordship in the campo de Montiel.

[3] Alcaraz, about fifty miles west of Valdepeñas, was taken on 22 May 1213; the king entered on the following day, 23 May. Rodrigo Jiménez de Rada was archbishop of Toledo.

[4] Riopar is about ten miles directly south of Alcaraz. Pentecost Sunday was 2 June.

gifts to the magnates, he summoned an incalculable host of people so that the king of León, stricken at least with fear, would make peace with the glorious king and, if he did not wish to help him against the Moors, at least would not interfere with him. Peace was thus established between the kings, through the mediation of Diego, and Pedro Fernández was expelled from both kingdoms.[5] For his part the king of León was bound to invade the land of the Moors; and so he did.

Fearing the inconstancy of the king of León, however, the glorious king assigned his vassal Lord Diego to him; he followed him with at least six hundred knights. They then attacked Alcántara and took it, fortified it, and kept it.[6] They then encamped before Mérida. While the king of León remained there for some days with his army, he then returned to his kingdom, despite Lord Diego's opposition and arguments to the contrary.

In view of the inconstancy and weakness of the king of León, the glorious king's noble vassal, who had heard that his lord, the glorious king, had also besieged Baeza (which had already been rebuilt and its walls repaired), did not wish to return to his land without his lord. Instead he traveled through deserted mountains and rough forest places, passing by the castles of the Moors, who opposed and resisted him; but he reached his lord, the glorious king, at the town mentioned above, where the siege was already established.

At the time when the king of León, or rather Lord Diego, captured Alcántara, the glorious and noble king had recently risen from his sickbed, where he had almost been at death's door. Although he could not ride at all by himself without the help of someone on whom he could support himself, he went to Toledo. With the very firm intention of ending his life in time of war in the land of the Moors, he besieged the town of Baeza with a few nobles and a few men from the people of the cities and other towns. This was done at the beginning of the month of December, and the siege lasted until after the feast of the Purification [2

---

[5] Diego López de Haro, lord of Vizcaya. Pedro Fernández de Castro, the son of Fernando Rodríguez, known as the Castilian, had participated with the Muslims in the battle of Alarcos against Alfonso VIII. Though he regained favor, the suspicion that he had encouraged Alfonso IX to ally himself with the Almohads after the battle of Las Navas de Tolosa was the reason for his expulsion from both kingdoms. He died in Morocco in 1214. See below, chap. 28, n. 3.

[6] Alcántara, on the Tagus river, about fifty miles west of Cáceres, was taken in 1213. It subsequently became the seat of the Military Order of Alcántara. See Joseph F. O'Callaghan, "The Foundation of the Order of Alcántara, 1176–1218," *Catholic Historical Review* 47 (1962): 471–486, repr. in *The Spanish Military Order of Calatrava and its Affiliates*, no. IV.

February 1214]. But lacking food and other necessities for the army, the noble king was forced to withdraw from the siege and to return to his land.

Indeed, so great was the shortage of food during that expedition that the meat of asses and horses was sold very dearly in the market. In fact, in that year there was such a famine in the kingdom of Castile, especially in Trasierra and Extremadura, as had never been seen or heard in those lands since ancient times. Indeed, people died en masse, so that there was hardly anyone to bury them.[7]

A truce was then established between the king of Morocco and the noble king of Castile. Indeed, there remained in the kingdom of Castile few horses and few other beasts of burden; a great number of people died, consumed by hunger. The Moors, on the contrary, had a great abundance of horses, wheat, barley, oil, and various other kinds of foods. Thus the land was quiet,[8] and the king rested and at the next Lent returned to Castile where he remained until the beginning of the following September.[9]

---

[7] Psalms 79:3: "They have poured out their blood like water round about Jerusalem, and there is no one to bury them"; 1 Maccabees 7.17: "There was no one to bury them"; Jeremiah 14:16: "There shall be none to bury them" (Douay).

[8] Psalms 76(75):9: "The earth feared and was silent"; 1 Maccabees 1:3: "The earth fell silent before him"; Habbakuk 2:20: "But the Lord is in his holy temple; silence before him, all the earth!"

[9] The king abandoned the siege in February 1214: Lomax, *The Reconquest of Spain*, 129–131.

27. THE BATTLE OF MURET AND
THE DEATH OF PEDRO II, 1213

At that time King Pedro of Aragón left his realm with a host of knights and set out for the region of Toulouse to aid the elder count of Toulouse, who had married the king's sister. The count's son similarly had married the king's other sister. The French were then in the region of Toulouse and held almost the entire viscounty of Bigorre and the greater part of the county of Toulouse.[1]

In fact, the Roman Pope Innocent III had given a general remission of all sins to all those who would go against the Albigensians and other heretics who were in those regions. For they had spread abroad various heresies, under various guises, but with like consequences. They were multiplying daily so much so that it was dangerous for the universal church to ignore the situation any longer.[2]

Therefore, Catholics came from various regions and especially from the kingdom of France, and in a short time subjected to the faith of Christ almost that entire area. In a moment of time they seized many castles and strongly-fortified though seemingly impregnable cities; they afflicted the heretics themselves with different penalties and put them to death in various ways. Indeed the power of our Lord Jesus Christ, who is King of kings and Lord of lords,[3] worked manifestly and miraculously through the ministry of the most illustrious and most faithful Count Simon de Montfort, who, like another Judah Maccabee, zealous for the law of God, manfully and powerfully fought the battles of the Lord.[4]

The king of Aragón and the count of Toulouse and other counts with them and barons and nobles of the land and many people, firmly believing that they would be able to capture him, besieged Count Simon de Montfort, who had scarcely five hundred knights with him, in a certain castle. But Count Simon was a brave and warlike man whose heart trusted firmly in the Lord Jesus Christ for

---

[1] Count Raymond VI of Toulouse had married King Pedro's sister, Leonor; her sister Sancha married the future Count Raymond VII. See Bisson, *The Medieval Crown of Aragon*, 38–39.

[2] The assassination of the papal legate, Peter of Castelnau, in 1208 prompted Innocent III to issue a bull of crusade against the Albigensians. Albigensianism or Catharism was a revival of the dualism of the Manichaean heresy. The count of Toulouse and other secular lords in the region were thought not to have been vigorous enough in opposing the heresy.

[3] Revelation 19:16: "King of kings and Lord of lords"; also 1 Timothy 6:15.

[4] Under the leadership of Simon de Montfort the crusaders swept through Languedoc from 1209 onward. For the biblical comparison see 1 Maccabees 3:1–9, esp. verse 2.

whom he labored daily. Thus, seeing the imminent danger to himself and to his people, in the power of the Lord Jesus Christ they left the castle under siege and rushed upon the camps. Through the strength of the Cross they forced them to flee and they killed the king of Aragón and many knights.[5] How happy that king would have been, if he had ended his life immediately after the noble triumph in the battle fought at Las Navas de Tolosa against the king of Morocco.

---

[5] Given Count Raymond VI's failure to support the crusade, Count Simon attacked his lands. Raymond's brother-in-law, Pedro II of Aragón, came to his aid, but they were defeated in the battle of Muret on 12 September 1213, and Pedro was killed. See O'Callaghan, *Medieval Spain,* 249–253; Jonathan Riley–Smith, *The Crusades. A Short History* (New Haven: Yale University Press, 1987), 133–139.

28. THE DEATH OF ALFONSO VIII AND QUEEN LEONOR, 1214

Meantime, about the beginning of the month of September, the glorious and noble king of Castile left Burgos and set out for Extremadura. There he planned to have a meeting with his son-in-law, the king of Portugal, in the district of Plasencia.[1]

But when he arrived at Valladolid, a messenger came unexpectedly to tell him of the death of his most noble and faithful vassal Lord Diego.[2] He mourned his death inconsolably, because he loved him and trusted him above all living beings. When he [the king] realized that the danger of death was already upon him, because he was already very weak and troubled by old age and worn out by many labors and sorrows, he had intended to entrust his kingdom and his son, who had not yet reached puberty, and his wife and daughters to the care of that noble and faithful vassal, leaving everything at his command and power, with the certain assurance that he would tend to everything faithfully and would quickly pay all his debts to the many to whom he was bound by obligation. Frustrated therefore in such a great hope and finding himself at death's door, the glorious king was saddened beyond measure.

A few days before he had heard of the death, in the land of Morocco, of Pedro Fernández, the Castilian, whom the noble king had pursued as his principal enemy.[3] And so, as happiness turns to sorrow and sorrow turns to joy, no one, while he is in this present life, can rejoice in being happy.[4]

After recovering his spirits, the glorious king continued on ahead. But when he reached a certain village called Gutierre Muñoz, between Arévalo and Ávila, he slowly began to decline. Around midnight, attended by a few members of his household, he entered upon the way of all flesh.[5] Meantime, his noble wife was then suffering from quartan fever.

May a dark whirlwind seize that night![6] May the stars of the sky not illumine

---

[1] Afonso II of Portugal was married to Alfonso VIII's daughter, Urraca, in 1208. Plasencia lies about fifty miles north of Cáceres and about one hundred and ten miles west of Toledo.

[2] Diego López de Haro, lord of Vizcaya, died on 16 September 1214.

[3] Pedro Fernández de Castro died on 18 August 1214 in Morocco.

[4] This is the classical tag "Count no man happy until he is dead", subtly christianized.

[5] The king died at midnight 5–6 October 1214. Ávila is about fifty miles northeast of Madrid; Arévalo is about twenty-five miles north of Ávila.

[6] Job 3:6: "May a darksome whirlwind seize upon that night" (Douay).

it,[7] because it dared to deprive the world of such a sun! He was the flower of the kingdom, the adornment of the world, conspicuous for every probity of morals, just, prudent, brave, generous; in no way had he stained his glory. He died on the eighth day after the feast of St. Michael. Lord Diego had died around the feast of the Exaltation of the Holy Cross.[8] For as long as this world will last, Castile has reason for perpetual sorrow, losing at one and the same time such a great lord and king and such a great man and such a very renowned vassal.

Those who were with the king at that time, namely, his wife and daughter, the archbishop of Toledo and the bishop of Palencia and other nobles, hastened to take his body, now deprived of life, to the royal monastery that the king himself had recently constructed at his own expenses outside Burgos.[9]

On hearing of the death of such a great lord, people from the cities and nobles gathered from everywhere; realizing that they had lost such a great king they were stupefied, groaning within themselves in distress of spirit. All the women broke out in lamentation, while the men put ashes on their heads and donned hairshirts and put on sackcloth.[10] All the glory of Castile was suddenly changed as in the blink of an eye.[11]

Then after the body of the glorious king was given magnificent and honorable burial, his noble wife, Queen Lady Leonor, deprived of the solace of such a great man, wished to die because of sorrow and anxiety of spirit. She soon fell into her sickbed, and on the vigil of All Saints [31 October 1214] around midnight, following her husband, she ended her last day. She was buried next to the king in the monastery already mentioned. The same burial place guards those whom one mind had joined and nobility of customs had adorned.

---

[7] Job 3:4: "May that day be darkness; let not God above call for it, nor light shine upon it!" Also cf. Wisdom 17:5b: "Nor did the flaming brilliance of the stars succeed in lighting up that gloomy night."

[8] The feast of St. Michael is September 29; the king died at midnight 5–6 October. The feast of the Exaltation of the Holy Cross is 14 September; Diego died on 16 September.

[9] Queen Leonor, the Infanta Berenguela, Archbishop Rodrigo of Toledo, and Bishop Tello of Palencia interred the king at Las Huelgas de Burgos, a convent of Cistercian nuns which he had founded about 1187.

[10] Lamentations 2:10: "They strew dust on their heads and gird themselves with sackcloth"; Jonah 3:5–6: "They proclaimed a fast and all of them, great and small, put on sackcloth . . . [the king] covered himself with sackcloth, and sat in the ashes."

[11] Cf. 1 Corinthians 15:52: "in an instant, in the blink of an eye."

When the glorious and noble king began to reign he was a child of scarcely three years of age. He reigned for nearly fifty years or more. He died in the era 1252 [A.D. 1214].[12]

---

[12] Alfonso VIII was born on 11 November 1155 and succeeded to the throne on his father's death on 31 August 1158. Thus he was not quite three when he became king. He reigned for nearly fifty-six years.

29. THE CRUSADE OF EMPEROR FREDERICK BARBAROSSA

Around the thirtieth year of his reign, the holy city of Jerusalem and all the Holy Land beyond Tyre, in the vernacular called Sur, and beyond Tripoli, which is in the region of Antioch, was taken.[1] Saladin, the sultan of Damascus and Babylon, fought against the king of Jerusalem and the friars of the Hospital and the Temple and, with the permission of divine justice, overcame them and killed many of them, though others were captured. Aside from the cities mentioned above, he seized the whole land. He also captured the Holy Cross of the Lord, which was taken in that battle.[2] The whole Christian people, on hearing this, mourned beyond measure, and the Roman pope sent his preachers to all the princes of the Christian people to invite them to liberate the Holy Land.[3]

Now Frederick, emperor of the Romans, whom all the princes of Germany followed, took the sign of the cross. Together with an innumerable multitude of knights and other warriors he passed through Hungary, then through Bulgaria, and then through Romania; and, overcoming and executing all those who wished to oppose him and his army so they could not pass, he reached the land of the sultan of Iconium, which touches on the land of the prince of Antioch.[4]

As report had it, he had the firm intention of going first against Damascus and Babylon to destroy the whole realm of Saladin and to subject it to the Christians, and then to enter the Holy Land and the holy city of Jerusalem with glory and honor. Although the earthly emperor proposed this, the King of kings and Lord of lords,[5] "in whose hand are all the powers and all the rights of kingdoms,"[6]

---

[1] Saladin conquered Jerusalem on 2 October 1187 and then overran the greater part of the kingdom of Jerusalem, except for Tyre where the crusaders held out. The cities of Tripoli and Antioch also continued under crusader rule. See Riley–Smith, *The Crusades,* 109–113.

[2] In the battle of Hattin on 3 July 1187 Saladin defeated King Guy of Lusignan who was taken prisoner together with the relic of the True Cross.

[3] Pope Gregory VIII issued a bull launching the Third Crusade on 29 October 1187.

[4] The principality of Antioch, lying just north of the County of Tripoli and the kingdom of Jerusalem, was one of the Crusader states.

[5] Revelation 19:16: "King of kings and Lord of lords"; also 1 Timothy 6:15 (quoted above, chap. 27, n. 3).

[6] This is a direct quotation from the prayer for the emperor in the Good Friday liturgy: "Omnipotens sempiterne Deus, in cuius manu sunt omnium potestates et omnia jura regnorum." Cf. Sirach 10:4: "Sovereignty over the earth is in the hand of God" (quoted above, chap. 5, n. 1).

disposed otherwise. For when he [Frederick] came to the boundaries of Iconium near Antioch, he wished to bathe in a certain small river because it was summer; he entered the water and suddenly was drowned there.[7] Behold, the judgments of God are an immense abyss.[8] Part of his army died but the other part turned their face toward the places that the Christians still held within the bounds of the Holy Land.

---

[7] The Holy Roman Emperor, Frederick I, known as Barbarossa (1152–1190), responded to the papal plea and set out in May 1189, marching through Hungary, the Byzantine Empire, and Anatolia (modern Turkey), then under the rule of the sultan of Iconium. On 10 June 1190 while swimming in the river Göksu he was drowned and his crusade came to an abrupt end. See Charles M. Brand, "Frederick I Barbarossa," in *Oxford Dictionary of Byzantium* (hereafter *ODB*), 3 vols. (New York: Oxford University Press, 1991), 2:804.

[8] Psalms 36(35):7: "Your justice is like the highest mountains, your judgments, like the mighty deep."

30. THE THIRD AND FOURTH CRUSADES.
THE FOURTH LATERAN COUNCIL

At the same time, Philip, king of the French, and Richard, king of the English, after establishing mutual peace between themselves, crossed over the sea with dukes and counts and many other barons and knights, and landed at Acre, which the Saracens still held. The kings forcefully besieged it; vigorously attacking it, they took it by force. Now King Richard, before he came there, seized the Island of Cyprus and subjugated it to himself.[1]

King Philip, however, suffering from a very grave illness, so much so that his life was despaired of, crossed the sea again and returned to his kingdom. But King Richard, brave and high-spirited, remained and stayed there for a long time in that region, defending what the Christians held and newly acquiring other [places].[2] But when he heard that the king of France wished to make war against him, he crossed the sea; but while he was traveling through the land of the duke of Austria, commonly called Esterrichia [Österreich], he was captured by the duke and held in captivity for a long time. At length, after 100,000 marks of silver were paid for his liberation, he returned to his kingdom. While besieging a certain castle, he was wounded mortally by an arrow and paid the debt of nature, as reported above.[3]

Around the fortieth year of the glorious king's reign, the count of Flanders and the count of Blois and other barons of the kingdom of France sent into Italy for the marquess of Montferrat, whom they appointed over themselves, firmly prom-

---

[1] Philip II Augustus (1180–1223) and Richard I the Lionheart (1189–1199) took the crusader's vow in 1188. In July 1190 they set out, sailing to Sicily where they spent the winter; in late March 1191, Philip sailed directly to Acre, while Richard on 5 June landed at Cyprus, then under the control of the Byzantine Isaac Comnenus, and took possession of the island. Cyprus thus became part of the crusader lands in the eastern Mediterranean. The king of Jerusalem, Guy of Lusignan, had begun the siege of Acre which Philip and Richard now joined. See Riley–Smith, *The Crusades*, 113–118.

[2] The crusaders captured Acre on 12 July. Philip sailed for home on 31 July. Richard's efforts to recover Jerusalem were thwarted by Saladin.

[3] Richard concluded a truce with Saladin in September 1192 and sailed for Europe on 9 October. On his way home he was shipwrecked and tried to make his way in disguise through Austria, whose duke he had offended during the Third Crusade. Captured, he was released early in 1194 only after his English vassals raised the ransom of 150,000 marks (more than our chronicler records). Once back in France he resumed his conflict with Philip Augustus, but he was killed in a quarrel with one of his vassals in 1199. See chap. 17.

ising to obey him as lord. Indeed they had agreed among themselves that they would go oversea to serve the Lord Jesus Christ.[4]

Thus all assembled at Venice. After they stayed there for a long time, on account of the malice and fraud of the Venetians,[5] Alexius, emperor of Constantinople, came to them. He was the son of Emperor Isaac, who had killed Andronicus, a most notorious traitor, as report has it; after the death of Emperor Manuel he had usurped the empire of Constantinople for himself through violence and treason.[6] Now Emperor Isaac was the grandfather of our lady Queen Beatriz, that is, the father of her mother.[7] Thus Alexius, making the miserable complaint that his subjects had unjustly deprived him of his empire, came and begged them humbly to deign to aid him out of a sense of pity. If perhaps through their aid he was able to recover the empire, he would generously provide the Franks and Lombards with everything necessary for the relief of the Holy Land.[8]

Overcome therefore by pity and driven by poverty they followed him. Out of fear of them the people of Constantinople received their lord, feigning an outward

---

[4] In 1198 Pope Innocent III launched the Fourth Crusade, whose leaders were Count Baldwin of Flanders, Count Thibault of Champagne, and Boniface, marquess of Montferrat. On their behalf Geoffrey de Villehardouin concluded a treaty with Venice in April 1201 to transport the crusaders by sea to the Holy Land. See Donald E. Queller and T. E. Madden, *The Fourth Crusade. The Conquest of Constantinople, 1201–1204*, 2d ed. (Philadelphia: University of Pennsylvania Press, 1997).

[5] Because the crusaders who came to Venice were unable to pay the sum agreed upon, the Venetians refused to sail. As a condition of taking them to the Holy Land, Venice persuaded the crusaders in November 1202 to join in the conquest of the Christian port of Zara on the Adriatic coast, which Venice perceived as a rival.

[6] The Byzantine Emperor Manuel I (1143–1180) was succeeded by his son Alexius II (1180–1184), but his cousin Andronicus Comnenus (1184–1185) made himself co-emperor. Andronicus was overthrown and killed by Isaac Angelus (1185–1195). Isaac, in turn, was ousted and blinded by his brother Alexius III (1195–1203). Isaac's son, the future Alexius IV, tried to enlist the crusaders in his cause. See Joan M. Hussey, *The Byzantine World* (New York: Harper, 1961), 60–71; Charles M. Brand, *Byzantium Confronts the West, 1180–1204* (Cambridge, Mass.: Harvard University Press, 1968; 2d ed., Aldershot: Gregg, 1992).

[7] Beatriz, the wife of Fernando III, was the daughter of the Holy Roman Emperor Philip of Swabia and Irene, the daughter of Isaac Angelus. See Charles M. Brand, "Philip of Swabia," *ODB* 3:1653, and cf. stemmata on 1:98, and 2:1145.

[8] Alexius Angelus offered to provide the crusaders with money and troops for the conquest of the Holy Land, if they would assist him in recovering the throne of the Byzantine Empire. See Charles M. Brand, "Alexios IV Angelos," *ODB* 1:65–66.

loyalty, while inwardly they were full of guile.[9] When the Franks and Lombards, complaining that Emperor Alexius would not respond to them as he had promised, withdrew and sailed for the Holy Land, the people of Constantinople turned against their lord, Emperor Alexius, and deprived him of the submission and obedience they had promised and owed.[10]

In view of the wickedness of his subjects, Alexius sent his envoys after the Franks and the Lombards to recall them, which was done. They returned and landed near the city of Constantinople. Though they were very few in comparison to the multitude of the people of Constantinople, the Lord is powerful, whether with a few or with many,[11] when he wishes to triumph. Aided therefore by divine grace, without which they could do nothing,[12] they broke into the city by force; killing many of the inhabitants of the place on the right and on the left, they took the city and seized infinite spoils of gold, silver, precious stones, silk cloth, and various kinds of ornaments, which abounded in Constantinople more than in all the cities of the world.[13]

Baldwin, count of Flanders, was elected as emperor, while the marquess of Montferrat was made king in Salonica. A certain Venetian was elected as patriarch; I saw him consecrated in Rome in the church of St. Peter by the hand of Lord Innocent III.[14]

---

[9] The crusaders and Venetians sailed in April 1203 for Constantinople. They besieged the city from 24 June to 17 July when they took it by assault. Alexius III fled; Isaac Angelus was restored to the throne, but his son Alexius IV (1203–1204) was installed as co-emperor. See Charles M. Brand, "Isaac II Angelos," *ODB* 2:1012.

[10] Alexius IV was unable or unwilling to fulfill his promises to collaborate with the crusaders in the conquest of the Holy Land. In February 1204 the people of Constantinople rose in revolt, deposed and killed him. His father died a few days later. Alexius Murzuphlus was proclaimed as emperor. See Charles M. Brand, "Alexios V Doukas," *ODB* 1:66.

[11] 1 Samuel (1 Kings) 14:6: "It is no more difficult for the Lord to grant victory through a few than through many"; cf. 1 Maccabees 3:18: "It is easy for many to be overcome by a few."

[12] John 15:5: "I am the vine, you are the branches. Whoever remains in me and I in him will bear much fruit, because without me you can do nothing."

[13] In March 1204 the Venetians and crusaders made a pact to conquer Constantinople and to establish a Latin Emperor. Then on 6 April they launched a second assault on the city and took it on 13 April. The spoils were immense. See Queller and Madden, *The Fourth Crusade*.

[14] Baldwin of Flanders was elected as emperor, while Boniface of Montferrat became king of Thessalonica. The rest of the empire was divided among the other crusaders and the Venetians. The Venetian Thomas Morosini was elected as patriarch and was consecrat-

From that time the Latins obtained Constantinople, and the church of Constantinople (whose patriarch, not the one mentioned, but his successor, I saw in the Lateran Council convoked by Innocent III) obeyed the Roman church.[15] That Council was celebrated in the next year after the death of the glorious king. Present there were 420 bishops and 72 archbishops[16] and the patriarchs of Constantinople, Jerusalem, and Aquileia and Grado. There was an untold number of abbots and priors and others holding offices. This was held on the feast of All Saints.[17] On the ides of the month of July following Lord Innocent III, a good man, whose deeds God caused to prosper, entered upon the way of all flesh.[18]

---

ed by Innocent III in March 1205. See Charles M Brand, "Baldwin of Flanders," *ODB* 1:247–248, and idem, "Boniface of Montferrat," *ODB* 1:304–305; Alexander Kazhdan, "Thomas Morosini," *ODB* 3:2077.

[15] The patriarch of Constantinople to whom our author refers was Gervaise elected in November 1215.

[16] In his second edition of the text (1997) Charlo Brea gave the number of archbishops as 62 (reading LXII); but Cirot, Cabanes Pecourt, and Charlo Brea in his first edition of the *Crónica,* 46, and in the second edition of his translation (*Crónica,* 63) read the number as 72.

[17] The Fourth Lateran Council was summoned by Pope Innocent III on 13 April 1213 to meet on All Saints' Day, 1 November 1215. The patriarchs of Constantinople and Jerusalem were Latin, not Greek patriarchs. The patriarchates of Aquileia and Grado were located in northeastern Italy. See Alexander Kazhdan, "Innocent III," *ODB* 2:996.

[18] Innocent III died on 16 July 1216 rather than 15 July.

III. The Reign of Fernando III,
King of Castile–León (1217–1252)

31. ENRIQUE I, KING OF CASTILE, 1214–1217

After the glorious king's death (while his wife still lived, although she already suffered from the illness which caused her death), his son Enrique was raised up to the kingship and was received by all the Castilians and the prelates of the churches and the people of the cities, who kissed his hand in homage to him. Now the boy was of good inclination but he had not yet attained his twelfth year.[1]

Thus, when Queen Lady Leonor labored in her last illness, she commended her son King Enrique and the kingdom to her daughter, Queen Lady Berenguela.[2] Then after her mother's death, Queen Lady Berenguela took her brother King Enrique under her protection, and, together with the archbishop of Toledo and the bishop of Palencia,[3] administered the government of the realm for three months or a little longer.

But some indignant magnates began to conspire and to look for certain pretexts whereby, after taking the boy king from the power and custody of his sister and the prelates, they could rule the kingdom as they pleased. So it happened that the majority of the barons agreed that Álvaro Núñez should become the king's guardian and should direct the government of the realm.[4] Thus Queen Lady Berenguela was persuaded, in some way or other, that Álvaro Núñez should have the king and the kingdom, but that in all difficult and major affairs, he should ask the

---

[1] Enrique I was born on 14 April 1204; thus he was about ten and a half years old. For his reign see González, *Alfonso VIII,* 1:217–238; O'Callaghan, *Medieval Spain,* 335.

[2] Berenguela became queen after the death of her brother Enrique I in 1217.

[3] Archbishop Rodrigo Jiménez de Rada of Toledo and Bishop Tello of Palencia.

[4] Álvaro Núñez de Lara was the son of Count Nuño Pérez de Lara who died in 1177.

lady queen's counsel and consent, and should do nothing without her. Álvaro Núñez swore all this and did homage to the lady queen concerning this. Let him see to it whether he observed it.[5]

---

[5] Apparently these events took place early in 1215. This part of the text was written before Álvaro's death in 1218.

32. THE CIVIL WAR AND THE DEATH OF ENRIQUE I

Not many days after the king had been taken from the queen's power, the barons of the kingdom were divided among themselves, some, namely, Gonzalo Rodríguez[1] and his brothers and many others, adhering to Álvaro Núñez; and some reached a very firm agreement among themselves against them [. . .]. Not very long afterward, Álvaro Núñez was made a count; after that Gonzalo Núñez was also made a count.[2] The estate of the realm deteriorated daily and everyone worked not for the government of the kingdom but rather for its desolation.

Count Álvaro Núñez, led by the advice of certain persons, tried to unite Lady Mafalda, daughter of the king of Portugal, in marriage — de facto, since he could not do so de iure — to Enrique, king of Castile. Thus it was done.[3]

At that time very grave enmities existed between Count Álvaro and Lope Díaz and Rodrigo Díaz de los Cameros; the count and his brothers brought it about that the king made war on those nobles. That was also done.

At the same time when the king and the queen (of whatever sort she may have been) were at Miranda they separated from one another on the command of the lord Pope Innocent.[4] Then a certain agreement (a fraudulent one, not a true one) was made between Count Álvaro and his accomplices and other nobles.

Later, around the feast of the Assumption [15 August 1216], when all the magnates had assembled at Valladolid to discuss the establishment of peace among

---

[1] One of the principal officers of the royal court, the mayordomo mayor Gonzalo Rodríguez Girón belonged to one of the leading Castilian noble families.

[2] Cirot and Cabanes Pecourt read Gunsalvus Nunii; Charlo Brea omits Nunii, but in both translations he reads Gonzalo Núñez. The title of count was an honorific bestowed by the king. Álvaro appears as count in May 1215 and his brother Gonzalo so appears in June 1216.

[3] The marriage to Mafalda, the daughter of Sancho I and the sister of Afonso II of Portugal, took place before 29 August 1215. As she was twenty-one and he was only about twelve the marriage was probably not consummated. In any case, they were related within the prohibited degrees and so the marriage was canonically invalid, as our author points out.

[4] The author's comment, "the queen (of whatever sort she may have been)" ["illa regina qualis qualis"] (the last two words being bracketed in Charlo Brea's text), reflects his opinion that the marriage of Enrique and Mafalda was uncanonical. The king's sister Berenguela protested to Pope Innocent III, who ordered the pair to separate on the threat of excommunication. The royal itinerary places the king in Miranda de Ebro, about fifty miles east of Burgos, on 1 June 1216. The couple evidently separated sometime before the pope's death on 16 July 1216.

themselves, new dissension broke out among them; and then Gonzalo Rodríguez and his brothers, and all who were bound to follow him, and Alfonso Téllez and his brother, abandoned Count Álvaro, and all adhered to Queen Lady Berenguela. Similarly Lope Díaz, Rodrigo Díaz, Álvaro Díaz, and Juan González[5] all allied with one another against Count Álvaro and his brothers and his other relatives who supported him. So much dissension and discord broke out and developed between the parties as had never happened before in Castile.

Out of fear, therefore, Count Álvaro withdrew to the region of Toledo. When he passed through Extremadura, he won to himself the minds of the leaders who were in the cities and towns, and united them to him by an indissoluble bond; with their support, almost all Extremadura and the land of Trasierra supported him.[6]

Then in the following winter, when Queen Lady Berenguela sent to her brother one of her servants by whom she could assure herself of his condition and health, certain decayed vessels,[7] deceitful agents of Satan, who were with Count Álvaro, conceived a diabolical fiction, composing a certain cursed letter which they said they had found on the queen's emissary; by this they endeavored to prove, so that they would all incur the king's hatred, that Queen Lady Berenguela had plotted her brother's death with Gonzalo Rodríguez and Alfonso Téllez and some other magnates. Although they had tried this many times before, they had never been able to bring it off.

On this pretext they hung the queen's emissary on a gallows, hoping thus to denigrate the lady queen's reputation and that of the nobles who sided with her. But the just Lord, who loves justice, whose face sees equity;[8] who saves the blameless and the innocent;[9] who delivered Susanna from the hands of wicked judges;[10] He indeed freed from anxiety and exalted in a time of tribulation[11] the

---

[5] The nobles opposing Count Álvaro were Gonzalo Rodríguez Girón, Alfonso Téllez de Meneses, his brother Tello Alfonso, Lope Díaz de Haro, Rodrigo Díaz and Álvaro Díaz de los Cameros, and Juan González.

[6] Count Álvaro and the king journeyed through Extremadura to Toledo in the fall of 1216.

[7] Isaiah 32:7: "The vessels of the deceitful are most wicked" (Douay).

[8] Psalms 11:7: "The Lord is just and loves just deeds; the upright shall see his face."

[9] Cf. Numbers 14:18: "The Lord is slow to anger and rich in kindness, forgiving wickedness and crime; yet not declaring the guilty guiltless, but punishing children to the third and fourth generation for their fathers' wickedness."

[10] See Daniel 13.

lady queen, who was innocent and in no way guilty of such a great crime, and those who supported her.

Indeed, when the queen heard of the death of her envoy, and understood the diabolical conspiracy, and also realized that she and her sister, who was with her, were threatened with insult and dishonor, she withdrew from her father's monastery where she lived with her sister and went to the castle of Gonzalo Rodríguez, called Autillo. That nobleman most kindly received them and humbly and devotedly served them, placing himself, his people, and his goods at their disposal for as long as they stayed there, which was until the death of King Enrique.[12]

Now Count Álvaro and his men came with the king to Valladolid at the next Lent. Then after Easter he set out with knights and the men of Extremadura who supported him, and began to lay waste in the valley of Trigueros all the property of Gonzalo Rodríguez and his brothers and of the others who supported them; they set their houses on fire end cruelly ravaged their other property. Then they came to the castle called Montealegre and besieged it. Suero Téllez, who was inside, on seeing the king, surrendered his castle to him. Later making their way through the Tierra de Campos, they came to Carrión, where they stopped for some days. Thence they returned to Villalba del Alcor. Coming by night, they wounded Alfonso Téllez most gravely and seized his horses and arms. Protected by divine mercy, however, he escaped from their hands and withdrew to his own land, which Count Álvaro with the king and his supporters besieged. Although they besieged it for many days, nonetheless they could not take it. They retired from the siege and went to Palencia.[13]

Now Queen Lady Berenguela and all those who favored her were in Autillo

---

[11] Cf. 1 Samuel (1 Kings) 26:24: "As I valued your life highly today, so may the Lord value my life highly and deliver me from all difficulties"; Proverbs 11:8: "The just man escapes trouble, and the wicked man falls into it in his stead"; Psalms 9:10: "The Lord is a stronghold for the oppressed, a stronghold in times of trouble"; Psalms 46 (45):2: "God is our refuge and our strength, an ever-present help in distress."

[12] Berenguela lived in the monastery of Las Huelgas de Burgos, founded by her parents, where her sister Constanza was abbess. These events took place in 1217. Autillo was to the west of Palencia.

[13] Ash Wednesday, the beginning of Lent, fell on 8 February and Easter on 26 March. Count Álvaro marched northward from Valladolid to Carrión. Trigueros is about ten miles directly north of Valladolid, and Montealegre about twenty miles northwest. Carrion is about thirty miles north of Palencia. Villalba del Alcor, where Alfonso Téllez was besieged, is about fifteen miles southwest of Palencia.

and in the castle of Cisneros[14] and other neighboring towns. They were all in such great anxiety that they did not know what to do. At length they decided to surrender their land to the king, if they were unable to come to terms otherwise with Count Álvaro. That seemed almost impossible or at least difficult.

While King Enrique was playing in Palencia in his accustomed manner with noble boys who followed him, one of them threw a stone and seriously wounded the king on the head. Because of this wound the king reached the end of his life within a few days. Count Álvaro and his men took his body out of Palencia and placed it in a certain tower in the castle of Tariego. Thus King Enrique died before reaching the age of puberty, in the month of June, before completing the third year of his reign.[15]

---

[14] Cisneros is about twenty miles northwest of Palencia.

[15] Count Álvaro and the king came to Palencia in May; the king was killed there on 26 May 1217. His body was taken to Tariego, southeast of Palencia, but he was eventually buried in Las Huelgas de Burgos.

33. FERNANDO III IS SUMMONED FROM LEÓN

When she heard of her brother's death, although it was not yet publicized, Queen Lady Berenguela immediately sent her envoys, noble and powerful men, namely Lope Díaz and Gonzalo Rodríguez, to the king of León who was then at Toro,[1] so that by some pretext, by some artifice, they could extricate from his father's power, her oldest born son, Lord Fernando,[2] who was then with his father, and bring him to her. Her intention was, as truly appeared afterward, to give her father's kingdom to her oldest son; since no other masculine child of King Alfonso was still alive, it [the kingdom] belonged to the queen herself by reason of the fact that she was older than her other sisters. Moreover, it was announced that this had been the will of the glorious king [expressed] in a certain charter,[3] confirmed by his leaden seal, which had been issued in the curia celebrated at Carrión, and which had been found in the armarium of the cathedral of Burgos.

Thus the nobles went to the king of León and, finding a useful pretext by which they could achieve their wish, they brought the boy with great speed to his mother who was still residing at Autillo. Truly indeed was this a useful pretext, for if it had not been done so prudently, perhaps today the Castilians would not have their own king.[4]

The queen, then, after taking counsel with the magnates who were with her, went to Palencia, where mother and son were received honorably with a solemn procession by Bishop Lord Tello who then presided over the church of Palencia. Next they went to the castle of Dueñas and took it by force.[5] The magnates who were with the queen then had an interview with Count Álvaro, hoping that they could reconcile him to the queen, so that the kingdom could thus be pacified. But nothing was accomplished. The queen, therefore, and her supporters went to Valladolid where she was honorably received. Then, after holding diligent discussion, it seemed to all that they should cross the Duero and enter Extremadura.

---

[1] Toro is about fifty miles west of Valladolid.

[2] For the reign of Fernando III see Julio González, *Reinado y diplomas de Fernando III*, 3 vols. (Córdoba: Monte de Piedad y Caja de Ahorros, 1980–1986).

[3] Although the royal charter is not extant, it was likely drafted during the curia of Carrión in 1188. See above, chap. 11. See also O'Callaghan, *Medieval Spain*, 335–336.

[4] This sentence indicates that this section of the *Chronicle* was written before Fernando III, king of Castile, succeeded to his father's throne of León in 1230.

[5] Dueñas lies about five miles south of Palencia.

34. ALFONSO IX INVADES THE KINGDOM OF CASTILE

Intending to go to Segovia, they came to Coca,[1] but the inhabitants of that place refused to admit them into the town. There also it was intimated that the Segovians and the other people of Extremadura would not receive them. It was also insinuated that if they were not careful, Sancho Fernández, the king of León's brother, was following them with a host of knights to do them harm and to seize them if he could.[2] Turning about with great haste, therefore, they went to Valladolid, whence they had set out. Next they sent to Segovia where the people of Extremadura and those of Trasierra were gathered to discuss the replacement of the king. When they came to Segovia they found the men assembled and, by themselves and their friends, they persuaded them to assemble again at Valladolid to discuss the replacement of the king; and so it was done.

Now Count Álvaro, after the queen and her people had withdrawn from Dueñas, went personally to the king of León and promised him many things, which, however, by God's grace, he could not carry out. But he persuaded the king to gather an army and invade the kingdom of Castile; because the kingdom was vacant, he would be able to acquire all, or at least a great part, of the kingdom. The king of León agreed to the count's advice, and therefore gathered an army and captured Villa García, and then Urueña and Castromonte, and came to a certain town, called Arroyo, between Valladolid and Simancas, and there he encamped.[3]

---

[1] Coca is about thirty miles south of Valladolid and about forty-five miles north of Segovia.

[2] Sáncho Fernández, the son of Fernando II of León by his second wife Urraca López de Haro, was a half-brother of Alfonso IX.

[3] Alfonso IX had invaded the Tierra de Campos to the west of Palencia and Valladolid. Castromonte is about fifteen miles northwest of Valladolid. Villagarcía is about eight miles farther on, and Urueña is about eight miles southeast of Villagarcía. Simancas is about eight miles southwest of Valladolid.

35. THE ACCLAMATION OF FERNANDO III AT VALLADOLID

In fact, Castile then had a king, namely, Lord Fernando, the son of Lady Berenguela. For the people of Extremadura and those of Trasierra, assembled at Valladolid on the second day of the month of July, that is, the third day before the king of León came to Arroyo, discussed the replacement of the king; although different people thought differently, at last, He, by whom kings reign and princes rule,[1] not wishing to deprive Castile of the consolation of its own king, and wishing also to restrain the foolish pride and exaltation of the king of León, brought agreement out of the discord of disagreement.[2]

The people of Extremadura and the others, who had assembled outside the gate of Valladolid in a certain field, came quickly to the market and begged Queen Lady Berenguela to come out to that place with her sons. For so great was the crowd of people that the royal palace could not contain them. The noble queen, therefore, with her sons Fernando and Alfonso, and the bishops of Burgos and Palencia, and other men of religion, and the barons who supported her, went out to the place mentioned, where a crowd of people awaited her coming.[3]

One of the people, speaking for all, who were all agreed on this, recognized that the kingdom of Castile belonged by right to Queen Lady Berenguela and that everyone recognized her as Lady and Queen of the kingdom of Castile. Nevertheless, they all unanimously begged her to turn over to her oldest son, Lord Fernando, the kingdom which was hers by proprietary right, because she was a woman and could not bear the burden of governing the kingdom. Seeing what she had ardently desired, she willingly consented to their request and granted the kingdom to her son. He was acclaimed by all in a great shout: "Long live the king!" Then with great joy everyone went to the church of Saint Mary; there, giving thanks to God, all who were present, both the magnates and the people of the cities and

---

[1] Again Revelation 19:16: "King of kings and Lord of lords"; and here Proverbs 8:15–16: "By me kings reign and lawgivers establish justice. By me princes govern, and nobles, all the rulers of the earth."

[2] The Latin of this line, "discordiam discordantium ad concordiam reuocauit" is reminiscent of the title of Gratian's canon law collection, *Concordia discordantium canonum*, and perhaps is another indication of our author's canonical training. See introduction.

[3] Infante Alfonso, one of the closest collaborators of his brother, Fernando III, became lord of Molina; his daughter María de Molina married King Sancho IV of Castile. The bishops of Burgos and Palencia were Mauricio and Tello respectively.

other towns, kissed the hand of King Lord Fernando in homage; and so his mother returned to the palace of her father with honor and great joy. King Lord Fernando had just begun his sixteenth year.[4]

---

[4] Fernando III was probably born at Benavente on 24 June 1201. See O'Callaghan, "The Beginnings of the Cortes of León–Castile," 1524–1525.

36. THE WITHDRAWAL OF ALFONSO IX OF LEÓN

After this, when the queen and those who were with her heard that the king of León had come to Arroyo, the town mentioned above, they sent two bishops to him, those of Burgos and Ávila, to ask him to desist from disturbing his son, now the king of Castile.[1] But the king of León did not wish to hear their pleas. Rather, puffed up by the foolish glory that he had conceived of having the empire, as was said,[2] he crossed the Pisuerga and came to Laguna where he remained for some days. Then he directed his course toward Burgos, laying waste the land thereabout; he came as far as Arcos, intending to go to Burgos, with the hope, vain though it was, of taking possession of it.[3] In those days Lope Díaz was in Burgos with many noble and brave Castilians, ready to expose their lives, if necessary, to defend the city. When the king of León saw that he had conceived a vain hope and that he labored uselessly, he returned to his own land by another route.[4]

Meantime the queen was at Palencia with her son and his vassals. Fifty knights from Ávila, with their standard and well-supplied by the town council, and fifty knights from Segovia also came there to serve the king and the queen.

Now when the king of León had returned to his own land, the king and queen and their people left Palencia and went to Burgos; they sent two bishops, Mauricio of Burgos and Tello of Palencia, and other religious men to the castle of Tariego, to take the body of King Enrique from there to bury it with his parents. For Count Álvaro had already ordered that Enrique's body should be given up to his sister the lady queen; and so it was done. Then they went to Palencia where they were well received. From there they set out for the castle of Muño, which they besieged at once, and remained there with the king.[5]

---

[1] Bishops Mauricio of Burgos and Domingo of Ávila.

[2] Alfonso VII (1126–1157), king of Castile and León, had proclaimed himself emperor of Spain in 1135, but his separation of the two kingdoms made it impossible for his successors to claim the empire; according to our chronicler, Alfonso IX hoped to do just that.

[3] Laguna de Duero is about five miles south of Valladolid; Arcos is about the same distance south of Burgos.

[4] Matthew 2:12: "They [the Magi] departed for their country by another way."

[5] The castle of Muño was a few miles south of Burgos.

37. THE BURIAL OF ENRIQUE I AT LAS HUELGAS DE BURGOS

The queen together with the bishops and other religious men caused the body of her brother to be carried to the paternal monastery and honorably buried there. Then the queen returned to the castle of Muño; her vassals strongly and vigorously attacked it and took it by force and led away as captives the knights who were there. Moving on, they next took Lerma, and then Lara, and then returned to Burgos. The king and queen were then received in that city with a solemn procession with great honor and infinite joy. For the Lord God almost miraculously had delivered the city of Burgos from the hands of their enemies, and restored it to its true and natural lady. There the lady queen rewarded the knights, insofar as she was able, for she had already expended whatever gold and silver her father had left her at the end of his life.

Then, on the advice of Lope Díaz, they set out toward Belorado and Nájera where they were received by the people of the towns, but they were not able to take the *alcázares*, because the knights of Count Gonzalo Núñez held them. So they returned to Burgos.[1]

---

[1] Lerma is about twenty-five miles south of Burgos; Lara is about the same distance to the southeast; Belorado is about twenty-five miles and Nájera about fifty-five miles east of Burgos. Gonzalo Núñez de Lara was a brother of Count Álvaro. The *alcázar* was a citadel within a city or town.

38. THE SUPPRESSION OF COUNT ÁLVARO'S REBELLION

While they remained there, Count Álvaro and his brothers and all his supporters assembled a host of knights and passed by Tardajos, and then came through
Quintanaortuño, reaching Río Cerezo and then Villafranca.[1] Then, rising in the
morning, they fell upon Belorado and broke into it by force, seizing whatever
they could find there, killing some of the inhabitants, wounding others, and taking
others captive. Thus the town was reduced to ruin and desolation. They spared no
person or age. Returning then with victory and great booty, each one went to his
own place.

When they heard what the counts and their accomplices did in that town, the
king and the queen, his mother, and those who supported them were touched
inwardly by a fierce sorrow[2] and mourned. But the Most High, who is a patient
accountant,[3] witnessing from the height of his glory the damage that they did, inflicted on Count Álvaro and his followers a punishment wondrous for all the ages.
For on the tenth day, that is, the Wednesday of *quatuor temporum* in the month of
September,[4] when the king and queen and certain magnates left Palenzuela to go
to Palencia, they passed near Ferreruela where Count Álvaro was; they saw him
outside the town among the vineyards where he could see them going by.[5]

When Alfonso Téllez, on whom he had inflicted many vile injuries, saw him,
he said to his brother and the others who followed him — for they had gone on
ahead of the king and queen, armed and ready for battle — "There is Count
Álvaro; come, let us attack him." So they drew up in battle array against him.
When he saw that, he wanted to enter the town with his men; but as he was the

---

[1] Count Álvaro's itinerary took him from Tardajos, about ten miles southwest of
Burgos, northwards to Quintanaortuño and Río Cerezo and finally to Villafranca, about
twenty-fives miles east of Burgos.

[2] Genesis 6:6: "When the Lord saw how great was man's wickedness on earth . . . his
heart was grieved" (quoted above, chap. 4, n. 1; chap. 12, n. 5; chap. 19, n. 6).

[3] Sirach 5:4: "For the Lord bides his time" (quoted above, chap. 18, n. 6).

[4] 20 September 1217. *Quatuor temporum*, the Four Seasons, or Ember Days, were days
of fasting and prayer celebrated on the Wednesdays, Fridays (the fourth and sixth ferias),
and Saturdays after the third Sunday of Advent, the First Sunday of Lent, Pentecost Sunday, and the Feast of the Exaltation of the Holy Cross (14 September). On those days the
Church gave special thanks to God for the fruits of the earth.

[5] The royal itinerary was moving from Burgos in a southwesterly direction from Palenzuela, on the Río Arlanza, toward Herrera, which lies northeast of Palencia.

last one — for those who followed him had already entered — they came up to him and seized him and threw him from his horse into the mud — because it had been raining then — and so they brought him, caked in mud, as a prisoner before the lady queen. When the lady queen saw her mortal enemy, who had so often inflicted so many injuries on the queen and those who loved her, she gave thanks as much as she could to the Most High, for conferring such a great benefit on her.

After going to Palencia, they then set out for Valladolid, taking Count Álvaro as a prisoner with them and guarding him with great care. There he was detained for some days; after a lengthy discussion, in return for his release, he surrendered to the king and queen all the fortresses that he held as well as all the others of those who supported him, except Castrogeriz and Orcejón; his brother, Count Fernando, held those two castles. If his brother refused to restore them to the king, he [Count Álvaro] was bound by the pact to aid the king against him with a hundred knights until the king recovered those castles.[6] The fortresses which the king recovered in exchange for the liberation of Count Álvaro were: in Trasierra, Alarcón, and Cañete; north of the Duero, Tariego, Amaya, Villafranca, Cerezo, Pancorbo, the tower of Belorado, and some others, and Nájera which Lope Díaz took. Until they were handed over, Count Álvaro was in the custody of Gonzalo Rodríguez. Once they were given up, he was permitted to go free.[7]

Consequently, the king and queen went to Castrogeriz against Count Fernando who was preparing to rebel there, for he had many knights with him. He had prepared in the mill of the castle wheat, barley, wine, meats, and other things necessary for a long time for himself and those who were with him. Nevertheless, he was persuaded by wiser counsel to receive his king and lord, to whom he surrendered the castles that he held, and received them back from the king's hand and became his vassal.[8]

---

[6] Castrojeriz lies twenty-five miles west of Burgos; Orcejón was near Palencia.

[7] Alarcón is about thirty miles south of Cuenca, and Cañete about twenty-five miles east of Cuenca. Tariego is just southeast of Palencia; Amaya is about thirty miles northwest of Burgos. The other towns lie to the east of Burgos: Villafranca, about twenty-five miles; Cerezo, about thirty; Pancorbo, about forty; Belorado, about twenty-five; and Nájera, about fifty-five.

[8] Castrogeriz is about twenty-five miles west of Burgos. Fernando III was in Valladolid from 13 October 1217, and on 26 November 1217 concluded a truce with his father Alfonso IX; that may have prompted Count Fernando to return to his allegiance. By January 1218 he was listed among the confirmants to royal charters.

Thus, through the action of divine mercy, within six months the disturbance of the kingdom of Castile, which some expected would be perpetual, abated and the king and his mother began to exercise the office of king in all parts of his kingdom.[9]

---

[9] Six months from the death of Enrique I on 26 May 1217 would extend to about 26 November, when Fernando III and Alfonso IX concluded a truce.

39. THE DEATHS OF COUNT ÁLVARO AND COUNT FERNANDO

In the following summer, Count Álvaro and his brothers and accomplices, seeing themselves expelled from the kingdom, took refuge in the town called Valdenebro where they prepared to rebel again. The king and his mother and a host of knights came to Medina de Ríoseco. Not many days later it happened that the count and those who were with him abandoned that town, and joined the king of León. Then again, following their advice, the king of León made war against his son. At last, after the king of León had besieged Castrejón, a village of Medina, for many days, peace was made between father and son through the mediation of certain magnates of the kingdom of Castile.[1]

When the counts and those who were with them saw that they were deprived of the counsel and aid both of the king of León and the king of Castile, they lamented that they did not know where to go or what they ought to do. Then Count Álvaro fell into a sickbed at Toro; despairing of his life, he assumed the habit and the order of the friars of the Knighthood of Santiago, and so he died and was buried in Uclés. But Count Fernando went oversea with some of his vassals and relatives and went to the king of Morocco with whom he stayed for some time; but later both he and some others who had followed him died in Morocco. The count's body was then brought back and buried in the church of the Hospital of Puente de Fitero.[2]

---

[1] In the summer of 1218 the king was advancing on Valdenebro, lying east of Medina de Ríoseco, about twenty-five miles west of Palencia. Castrejón, a village belonging to Medina del Campo, is about thirty miles southwest of Valladolid. Fernando III and Alfonso IX concluded a permanent peace settlement on 26 August 1218: González, *Alfonso IX, 2*: 458–459, 479, nos. 350, 366.

[2] Count Álvaro became a knight of the Order of Santiago and was interred in its principal Castilian seat at Uclés (about sixty-five miles east of Toledo). His brother Count Fernando went off to serve the Almohads in Morocco in the early months of 1219. The Hospital of Puente de Fitero lay on the Río Pisuerga on the pilgrimage route to Santiago de Compostela.

40. THE MARRIAGE OF FERNANDO III
AND BEATRIZ OF SWABIA

In the following year Queen Lady Berenguela, whose whole intention and su-preme desire was to secure the honor of her son in every way, began to discuss finding a wife for her son. But as different people thought differently, it pleased the queen to arrange a marriage with the one who seemed to her to excel others in nobility of birth in the whole of Christendom. For at that time there was in Germany a most noble girl of great beauty and honorable habits for one of such an age, namely, the daughter of Philip, king of Germany, emperor-elect of the Ro-mans, the son of Frederick the Great, emperor of the Romans. The girl's mother was the daughter of Isaac, emperor of Constantinople; and so she was the grand-daughter of the two emperors who are considered the greatest and most distin-guished in the whole world.[1]

Thus, after the lady queen had sent other ambassadors to Germany about this affair, and had received letters from the king of Germany, the future emperor of the Romans,[2] to send more solemn ambassadors to accompany the young lady, she dispatched Mauricio, bishop of Burgos, Pedro Ovárez, prior of the Hospital, the abbot of San Pedro de Arlanza, the commander of Carrión, and García González, the former master of the Order of Uclés, that is, the Knighthood of Santiago.[3]

When they appeared before the king of Germany they were honorably received by him. After remaining in Germany for almost four months, at last they achieved their wish.[4] They brought the most noble and beautiful young lady, safe and sound, after the many dangers of such a long journey, to Queen Lady Beren-guela. Together with a noble company of religious men and ladies, she met the ambassadors and the young lady outside Vitoria. From there they went to Burgos,

---

[1] Beatriz of Swabia (born after 1198) was the daughter of Philip, emperor-elect (1198–1208), son of Frederick I Barbarossa (1152–1190), whom our author calls Frederick the Great. Her mother was Irene, the daughter of the Byzantine emperor Isaac Angelus. See chap. 30 above concerning the Fourth Crusade, with notes.

[2] Frederick II, elected as king of the Romans by the German princes in 1212 (and again in 1215), was crowned as Roman emperor by Pope Honorius on 20 November 1220. He was the son of Emperor Henry VI, a brother of Beatriz's father, Philip of Swabia.

[3] The first embassy to Germany probably took place in the fall of 1218. The second embassy probably set out for Germany in mid-1219. The abbot of San Pedro de Arlanza was Pedro. Other sources mention Juan, chamberlain of the monastery of San Zoilo de Carrión, and Rodrigo, abbot of the Cistercian monastery of Ríoseco.

[4] Horace, *Ars poetica*, 76: "uoti compos."

where the king was with his magnates and many other nobles and the chief men of the cities and towns of his kingdom. The king received the young lady and the ambassadors with great honor and joy.[5]

Then, on the third day before the feast of Saint Andrew, King Fernando, on his own authority, took, from the altar of the royal monastery which his grandfather and grandmother had built, the sword of war as a sign of knighthood. Bishop Mauricio of Burgos, after first solemnly celebrating mass there, had previously blessed it with other arms. There was great joy in the city on that day.[6]

Three days later, that is, on the feast of Saint Andrew [30 November], King Lord Fernando solemnly took as his wife the most noble young lady, Queen Lady Beatriz, in the church of Saint Mary at Burgos. Together with her he received the priestly blessing from the hand of Mauricio, bishop of Burgos.[7] A multitude of magnates, knights and chief men of the cities having been summoned, a most celebrated curia was held then in Burgos. Besides Queen Lady Berenguela, all the more noble ladies, both religious and secular, as many as there were in the kingdom of Castile, attended that curia. Such a curia had not been seen in the city of Burgos since ancient times.[8]

---

[5] The return journey was begun in the early fall. The company passed through Paris where Queen Berenguela's sister, Blanca or Blanche, was married to the future King Louis VIII of France. Vitoria, in Navarre, is about sixty miles northeast of Burgos.

[6] On 27 November 1219 Fernando III knighted himself in the Cistercian nunnery of Las Huelgas de Burgos, founded by Alfonso VIII and Leonor of Castile.

[7] The royal wedding took place in the cathedral of Burgos on 30 November 1219. See O'Callaghan, *Medieval Spain,* 335–336.

[8] O'Callaghan, "The Beginnings of the Cortes," 1525–1526.

41. THE REBELS: RODRIGO DÍAZ DE LOS CAMEROS AND GONZALO PÉREZ DE MOLINA

In the course of time, although Rodrigo Díaz de los Cameros had wanted to rebel against the king, at last he surrendered his land to him and received a certain sum of money; he wanted to go to the aid of the Holy Land. He had already been signed with the cross for many days.[1]

After another year had passed, Gonzalo Pérez de Molina, following counsel that was less than wise, with his supporters began to ravage and to plunder part of the kingdom near Molina. The king then, together with his most excellent mother, gathered his vassals and attacked Molina and laid waste the whole territory of the lord of Molina. Finally he besieged the castle of Zafra; once the siege was established Gonzalo Pérez saw that he could not resist the king's power, and acknowledged the lord king, and recognized whatever his grandfather, the most distinguished King Lord Alfonso, had held in Molina and (as it is said) even more.[2]

---

[1] Around 1220 the king summoned Rodrigo to his curia to give an account of his administration of certain tenancies; when he refused, the king confiscated them, but he later gave Rodrigo 14,000 *maravedís* as compensation. Rodrigo may have taken the crusader's vow with the intention of participating in the Fifth Crusade, under the aegis of the papal legate, Cardinal Pelagius, himself a Spaniard; or he may have done so as a means of protecting himself against the king. See Rodrigo Jiménez de Rada, *Historia de rebus Hispanie,* 291–292, Bk. 9, chap. 11.

[2] Gonzalo Pérez de Lara. lord of Molina, rebelled in the summer and fall of 1223. The settlement probably provided for the marriage of Gonzalo's daughter Mafalda and Fernando III's younger brother, Infante Alfonso. After Gonzalo's death in 1239, Mafalda and Infante Alfonso inherited the lordship. Molina de Aragón was situated on the frontiers of Castile and Aragón, about a hundred miles northeast of Madrid. Alfonso VIII was the grandfather of Fernando III.

42. THE MARRIAGE OF KING JOHN OF JERUSALEM AND THE PRINCESS BERENGUELA

In the seventh year of King Lord Fernando, King John of Jerusalem made a pilgrimage to Santiago; he came to take to wife one of the king of León's daughters: along with her the kingdom of León had been promised to him.

Nevertheless, the king sent his envoys on ahead to Queen Lady Berenguela and to the king, her son, who were then at Toledo, asking if they would be pleased to see him. It pleased the king and queen. So the king came to Toledo and was honorably received by the king and the queen. He discussed with them the marriage of the queen's daughter, the king's sister.[1] But like a prudent woman looking to the future, Queen Lady Berenguela foresaw the impediment that the king of Jerusalem might create for the right of her son, King Lord Fernando, to the kingdom of León, if the king [John] contracted marriage with either of the daughters of the king of León, whom he had had by Queen Lady Teresa, and if he should remain in that kingdom. She preferred to give her daughter, Berenguela by name, to the king as his wife.[2]

The queen promised, and on the return of the king from his pilgrimage the promise was fulfilled. Now that king was a man of great counsel, vigorous in arms, powerful in word and deed. A curia was celebrated therefore at Burgos, and the girl was solemnly handed over to the king as his wife. The king and his mother the queen and his wife accompanied the king of Jerusalem and his wife as far as Logroño and gave them generous gifts, commending them to the grace of God. They then returned to Burgos.[3]

---

[1] John of Brienne, king of Jerusalem, after first making inquiries, arrived in Toledo in April 1224; there he discussed his marriage to Berenguela's daughter, who was also the sister of Fernando III. He then went on to Santiago.

[2] Initially King John had intended to marry a daughter of Alfonso IX of León and his first wife, Teresa. If he had done so, he would have been able to claim the kingdom of León upon Alfonso IX's death. Berenguela wanted to assure the succession of Fernando III, her son by Alfonso IX.

[3] The wedding was solemnized in the curia of Burgos in May 1224. Logroño, on the Ebro, is about sixty-five miles east of Burgos; Fernando III and Berenguela had returned from there to Burgos by 2 June.

43. FERNANDO III PROPOSES TO GO TO WAR
AGAINST THE MOORS

After solemnly celebrating the feast of Pentecost at Burgos in the era 1252 [A.D. 1224], the king went out to a place called Muño. Lope Díaz, Gonzalo Rodríguez, Alfonso Téllez, Rodrigo Rodríguez, and almost all the magnates of the kingdom were then present in the royal court.[1]

On a certain day when the Spirit of the Lord rushed upon him,[2] the king, unexpectedly, humbly, and devoutly, as an obedient son, spoke in this manner in the presence of his most noble mother and all the magnates standing about:

Most beloved mother and most sweet lady: Of what benefit to me is the kingdom of Castile, which, though due to you by right, your generosity abdicated and granted to me; of what [benefit to me is] the most noble consort brought from distant lands through your solicitude and labor and joined to me in marriage with indescribable honor; of what [benefit to me is it that] you anticipate my desires with maternal sweetness, and before I have fully conceived them, you bring them to most brilliant effect: if I am dulled by laziness, if the flower of my youth is fading away without fruit, if the light of royal glory, which already had begun to shine like certain rays, is being extinguished and annihilated? Behold, the time is revealed by almighty God, in which, unless I want to pretend otherwise like a weak and deficient man, I am able to serve the Lord Jesus Christ, by whom kings reign,[3] against the enemies of the Christian faith, to the honor and glory of His name. The door is open indeed and the way is clear. Peace has been restored to us in our kingdom; discord and deadly enmities exist among the Moors; factions and quarrels have broken out anew. Christ, God and Man, is on our side; on that of the Moors, the infidel and damned apostate Muhammad. What is to be done? Most kind mother, from whom, after God, I hold whatever I have, I beg that it may please you that I wage war against the Moors.

---

[1] Pentecost fell on 2 June 1224. The king was at Muño, a few miles south of Burgos, on 6–16 June. The nobles were Lope Díaz de Haro, Alfonso Téllez de Meneses, and the brothers, Gonzalo Rodríguez Girón and Rodrigo Rodríguez Girón.

[2] Again cf. Judges 14:6: "But the Spirit of the Lord came upon Samson."

[3] Again Proverbs 8:15: "By me kings reign. . . ."

88

That said, the king, whose heart the Spirit of the Lord had inspired and aroused, was silent. All the barons who were present, were amazed, and, seeing the king's passion and glorious proposal, almost all were torn by immense joy.

44. QUEEN BERENGUELA'S RESPONSE.
PREPARATIONS FOR WAR AGAINST THE SARACENS

The noble queen, seeing that her son's heart was ardent and afire with such a noble desire, spoke a few words to her son, as was her custom:

Most sweet son, you are my glory and my joy! In my heart I have always wished for your happiness and success and, insofar as I was able, I have brought it about. Your vassals are here; the court is assembled. Let them counsel us as they are bound to do and you will follow their advice in this matter.

At the request of the magnates the king withdrew for a time, while they remained with the noble queen. After having a short discussion and deliberation, all agreed in this opinion: that the king should make war on the Saracens in every way. When the king learned of his mother's decision and heard the response of the magnates, he rejoiced in the Lord, more than could be believed.

Without delay the commander of Uclés was sent to the archbishop of Toledo and the master of Calatrava, who were in Trasierra, to attend personally upon the king, without any delay or offering any excuse, at Carrión, where the king would celebrate a curia concerning this affair.[1] Thus at the beginning of the month of July the king entered Carrión. There, together with his noble mother and the archbishop of Toledo and the bishop of Burgos and all the magnates of the realm, after discussion, the decision to make war against the Saracens was confirmed.

The king then commanded all the magnates and his other vassals and the Masters of the Orders to come to Toledo at the beginning of September next, prepared to invade Saracen territory with him. The king himself, like a roaring lion,[2] in fulfillment of his vow,[3] crossed through Extremadura and entered Toledo

---

[1] Pedro González, the commander of Uclés, was the second in command of the Military Order of Santiago. The Master of Calatrava was Gonzalo Yáñez. Rodrigo Jiménez de Rada was archbishop of Toledo.

[2] Ezekiel 22:25: "Her princes are like roaring lions that tear prey" (quoted above, chap. 12, n. 8).

[3] Horace, *Ars poetica*, 76: "uoti compos" (quoted above, chap. 40, n. 4). Charlo Brea, in his first translation of the *Crónica*, 63, translated the phrase "quasi uoti compos" as "como cumplidor de su voto" ["as one fulfilling his vow"]. His second translation of the *Crónica*, 75, reads: "como cumpliendo un voto" ["as if fulfilling a vow"]. I think the phrase suggests that the king took the crusader's vow in the curia of Carrión. The king was at Palencia on 16 July.

around the feast of the Assumption of Blessed Mary [15 August].

His barons and the archbishop and the friars of the Orders gathered with him. In the following September around the feast of St. Michael[4] they moved their forces against the Moors. Passing through the Puerto del Muradal, they hastened along the road toward the town called Quesada.[5] When they came upon it they entered the town in an instant; finding it full of riches, they plundered it of all its goods. They knocked down the walls to the ground, and took captive men and women, including older people and nursing mothers. Such a great number of people was found there that one would scarcely have believed beforehand.

---

[4] The Archangel Michael was revered as a warrior saint, so it was symbolic that the advance against the Moors was begun on his feast day, 29 September 1224.

[5] Quesada is about twenty miles southeast of Úbeda; the conquest was not definitive, for the Muslims soon reoccupied it.

45. CIVIL WAR AMONG THE ALMOHADS IN
MOROCCO AND SPAIN

At that time the king of Baeza sided with our king. For after being expelled from his own kingdom, that is, Jaén and Úbeda, and from the other towns that belonged to that kingdom, he lived in Baeza, because it alone remained to him.[1]

After the death of the king of Morocco, the son of the one whom Lord Alfonso, the most illustrious king of Castile, had routed in the battle fought at Las Navas de Tolosa, the kingdom of Morocco was vacant for some days, because the king, who left only sons under age, had not designated any heir for the kingdom. Thus opinions were divided in the Almohad court at Marrakech, which indeed up until that time had flourished for many days. One person was elected as king; but the others, who did not like him, assassinated him within a few days. For that reason so much discord broke out among the powerful men of that realm, that has not been capable of resolution even to this day, and it still goes on, and may it go on for ever. And so it was that each appointed a different man as king, for each person wished to have a lord of his own choosing, who, he hoped, would be advantageous to him.[2]

The discord that arose beyond the sea redounded in Spain, so that the king of Murcia was declared king of Morocco. Seville and the greater part of the land of the Saracens on this side of the sea favored him.[3] Now the king of Baeza and his brother who dominated Valencia and their supporters opposed the king of Murcia, who had already been proclaimed king of Morocco.[4] Thus a great division occurred between the Moors beyond the sea and on this side of the sea. One could more truly speak of dissension than of a kingdom, because it was well known that the Moroccan [kingdom] was collapsing.

---

[1] Abû Muhammad, commonly called al-Bayâsî, was governor of Seville under the Almohads before striking out on an independent course. Jaén, one of the principal towns of Upper Andalucía, is about fifty miles east of Córdoba and about forty north of Granada. Baeza is about twenty-four miles northeast of Jaén; Úbeda is about ten miles east of Baeza.

[2] Abû Ya'qûb Yûsuf, al-Mustansir (1213–1224), died on 6 January and was succeeded by his great-uncle 'Abd al-Wâhid, who was strangled on 7 September. On the succession crisis among the Almohads see Lomax, *The Reconquest of Spain,* 136–137.

[3] Al-'Âdil, governor of Murcia, the brother of the caliph, Muhammad ibn Ya'qûb, an-Nasir, who had died in 1213, proclaimed himself caliph in Spain and then crossed over to Morocco, where he was acknowledged after the strangulation of 'Abd al-Wâhid. He ruled from 1224 to 1227.

[4] Al-Bayâsî's brother Abû Zayd was governor of Valencia.

Indeed on this account everyone could know truly what the Prophet Daniel said: that "the kingdom of men is in the hand of God and he will give it to whomever he wishes."[5] The saying of the Prophet Isaiah was fulfilled: "Woe to you who plunder, will you not be plundered? and you who ravage, will you not be ravaged? when you finish plundering, you will be plundered."[6]

So also the *Mahdí*, who was called 'Abd al-Mu'min de hazedus,[7] who, on the preaching of Ibn Tûmart, a philosopher from Baghdad, deprived their Almoravid lords of their kingdom contrary to justice, and subjected to himself peoples and kingdoms, when he had accomplished these things, his descendants were deprived of his kingdom in our day by a jealous God, who visits the sins of the fathers on the children to the third and fourth generation.[8] May the name of the Lord be blessed.[9]

---

[5] Daniel 4:29: "The Most High rules over the kingdom of men and gives it to whom he will"; 5:21: "The Most High rules over the kingdom of men and appoints over it whom he will" (quoted above, chap. 14, n. 9).

[6] Isaiah 33:1: "Woe, O destroyer never destroyed, O traitor never betrayed! When you finish destroying, you will be destroyed; when wearied with betraying, you will be betrayed."

[7] Ibn Tûmart had proclaimed himself the *mahdí*, "the rightly-guided one," who would bring about the final victory of Islam. 'Abd al-Mu'min was the first Almohad caliph (1130–1163). The meaning of "de hazedus" is unknown. See chap. 6.

[8] Numbers 14:18: ". . . punishing children to the third and fourth generation for their fathers' wickedness"; Exodus 20:5: "For I the Lord, your God, am a jealous God, inflicting punishment for their fathers' wickedness on the children of those who hate me down to the third and fourth generation."

[9] Psalms 113(112):2: "Blessed be the name of the Lord, both now and forever."

46. FERNANDO III ATTACKS QUESADA, PRIEGO AND LOJA

Thus the king of Baeza made an alliance with our King Fernando, and gave his younger son to him to go with him to the kingdom of Castile so he [Fernando] would more completely trust the king of Baeza.

Because wintertime was coming on, our king returned to his own land with great joy and a lot of booty from the town of Quesada, which was entirely destroyed. Then the king of Valencia, the brother of the king of Baeza, sent his solemn envoys to our king, begging him to allow him to come to him. For he wished to see him and wanted to serve him in every way. Thus [Abû] Zayd of Valencia came to our lord the king at the town called Moya.[1] There, with everyone who was present looking on, he became the vassal of our lord the king and kissed his hand. A pact was concluded between them which [Abû] Zayd of Valencia, like a vile apostate, afterward violated for no just cause.

In the following year, in the era 1263 [A.D. 1225], our king returned to Castile and generously distributed stipends to his knights. Gathering a great and powerful army around the feast of St. John [25 June], at that time when kings are accustomed to go to war, he swiftly passed through the Puerto del Muradal. There the king of Baeza met him and, together with his sons, became his vassal and faithfully adhered to him until death.[2]

They broke camp and advanced. The army headed quickly toward Jaén and laid waste the land thereabouts, except that which belonged to the lordship of the king of Baeza. Then approaching the noble and famous city of Jaén, they besieged it and attacked it for many days, shutting up within all those who were in the town. They plundered the orchards and vineyards and trees and crops. The face of that noble city, flourishing and vigorous, was blackened darker than coal;[3] the land wilted, and the fields were abandoned. Its previous glory decayed, decayed.[4] The king and those who were with him realized that they could not take it by force because it was very strong and well fortified by nature and artifice; from there they decamped toward other towns, namely Priego and Loja, which they

---

[1] Moya is about fifty miles east of Cuenca and about sixty miles west of Valencia.

[2] Fernando III was in Burgos in March and in Toledo in May 1225. Al-Bayâsî formally declared himself Fernando III's vassal at Las Navas de Tolosa.

[3] Lamentations 4:8: "Now their appearance is blacker than soot."

[4] Cf. 1 Samuel (1 Kings) 4:21: "Gone is the glory from Israel." See also Rabanus Maurus, *Enarrationes in Epistolas B. Pauli*, 13.11, PL 112:225B.

took by force; they plundered all their goods, killed many thousands of Moors and captured many.[5]

Then they moved their army against the most noble city called Granada. They discovered, however, a certain town, great and strong, but evacuated by the people out of fear of the king and his army. There they found plentiful provisions and some other things; when they withdrew they left it entirely desolate. Approaching the city of Granada, they did not inflict much damage on that city. Seeing that they lacked victuals for the army, they decided, after leaving all that land in desolation, to return by another route to the land of the Christians.[6]

---

[5] Priego is about thirty-five miles northwest and Loja is about thirty miles directly west of Granada; these towns were not permanently occupied.

[6] See Lomax, *The Reconquest of Spain*, 137–138.

47. THE CASTILIANS AND THE KING OF BAEZA
CAMPAIGN IN ANDALUCÍA

Passing by Jaén, they completely destroyed whatever had remained intact in that region; and thus they came to the river Betis which in Arabic is called the Guadalquivir. When all the people withdrew from that place to their land, the king remained with his nobles, that is, the magnates, and other knights. Then the king of Baeza, according to the pact that he had concluded with our king, surrendered to him Martos, a noble castle well fortified by nature, Jaén, Andújar, and some other minor castles.[1] For he was obliged by the pact to yield to our king all the fortresses that he wished to receive, and to keep in the land of the Moors those which the king of Baeza could hold.

Then Álvaro Pérez, a young noble, the son of Pedro Fernández, who had already given up his friendship with the Moors, became a vassal of our king and received those castles from the king's hand; for a long time thereafter he faithfully and powerfully held and defended them.[2]

Moreover, the Master and friars of Calatrava and the commander and friars of Uclés and some other nobles remained at that time on the frontier. Together with the king of Baeza, to whom many knights called *alavares*[3] were already attached, they all inflicted much damage on the Saracens. As things were thus disposed, our king returned with joy and great glory to Toledo to his mother and his wife who were dwelling there at that time. The Master and his friars, the commander and his friars, and Álvaro Pérez and Rodrigo Rodríguez, together with their knights, descended into the area of Seville. There they engaged the army of the king of Seville, who ruled in Seville on behalf of al-Miramamolín; defeating them and chasing them from the field, they killed many Moors in the battle.[4] Then almost all the towns and castles between Córdoba and Seville went over to the king of Baeza and received him as lord. At last, Córdoba, a noble and famous city, received him as king and submitted to his lordship; their own king, the brother of the king of Seville, was seized and put in chains.[5]

---

[1] Martos is about twelve miles west and Andújar about thirty-five miles northwest of Jaén. Al-Bayâsî did not have control of Jaén, so nothing came of this.

[2] Álvaro Pérez de Castro, like his father, had been in the service of the Almohads.

[3] *Alavares* probably means *almogávares*, lightly armed soldiers, usually foot soldiers.

[4] Al-Miramamolín was the Caliph al-'Âdil, whose brother Abû-l-'Ulâ was governor of Seville. The Christians gained the victory at Aznalcázar, about fifteen miles southwest of Seville.

[5] See Lomax, *The Reconquest of Spain,* 138–139.

48. FERNANDO III REQUIRES THE KING OF BAEZA
TO YIELD SALVATIERRA, BURGALIMAR, AND CAPILLA

At that time, the noble knight Alfonso Téllez, the bishop of Cuenca, and the towns of his diocese, invaded the territory of Murcia.[1] There, after besieging a certain castle, they gave battle to an innumerable array of almost all the Moors on that frontier. Through the power of our Lord Jesus Christ they overcame the Moors and killed many thousands of Moors in that battle. The Lord of Valencia, who is named [Abû] Zayd, breaking his alliance without reason, had already withdrawn from the suzerainty and friendship of our king.

Stirred by the Spirit of God,[2] the king, holding firmly and irrevocably to the aim of destroying that cursed people, decided to return to that region around the feast of All Saints [1 November 1225] to visit and console the Master of Calatrava and the others whom he had left on the frontier. Almost all his magnates and counselors opposed his intention, not because they wished to be inactive through sloth or idleness; rather they feared that, because of the harshness of winter and the flooding of rivers, the king's plan for the coming summer would be ruined; it was feared that on account of the scarcity of knights and other men he would not be able to do any damage to the Moors and he himself and his men would be harmed.

Nevertheless, the king, into whom the Spirit of the Lord had come,[3] followed wiser counsel, as if from the Spirit of the Lord, and put aside — I will not say rejected — the opinion and counsel of everyone. The glorious knight of Christ set out rapidly from Toledo and began to head toward that territory.

When he came to that area he sent his solemn envoys to the king of Baeza who was then in Córdoba, which he had entered a few days before as the new king and lord, to put aside all other business and to come to him in the land of Andújar, where our king then was. After receiving the envoys and honoring them with generous gifts, the king of Baeza obeyed the command of his lord and gathered a great host of knights and foot soldiers and came to our lord the king.

Seeing that multitude, some of our noblemen, brave in arms and great in counsel, were very much afraid; they suspected that the treachery of those people — who saw ruin threatening them — had prepared a trap for the king and his people. The king, however, remained unperturbed. Exercising his power of com-

---

[1] Lope, who appears as bishop-elect of Cuenca in 1225, was recorded as bishop on 22 February 1226.

[2] Judges 14:6: "But the Spirit of the Lord came upon Samson."

[3] See the previous note.

mand, he required the king of Baeza as his vassal, according to the pact written and confirmed between them, to surrender to him those fortresses, which he would choose in the kingdom of Córdoba that he [the king of Baeza] had recently acquired.

Then the king of Baeza and Córdoba, inasmuch as he did not trust the Moors and had placed all his hope in our king, promised to give him immediately the famous castle of Salvatierra, as well as Burgalimar and Capilla. To fulfill these promises he yielded the *alcázar* of Baeza at once to the Master of Calatrava, so that, if he did not fulfill his promises, the Master could surrender the *alcázar* of Baeza to our king without any dishonor or bad faith.[4]

---

[4] The *alcázar* was the citadel of Baeza. Burgalimar is about forty miles south of Salvatierra and about the same distance to the north of Baños de la Encina. Capilla is about fifteen miles west of Almadén which is about forty miles west of Ciudad Real. See Lomax, *The Reconquest of Spain*, 139.

49. THE SIEGE OF CAPILLA AND
THE MURDER OF THE KING OF BAEZA

Then, after confirming their first pact and fortifying the castles which our king had recently acquired, and having established the Master of Calatrava and his friars in the *alcázar* of Baeza, our king and the king of Baeza went their separate ways. Our king began to return to Toledo and then the castle of Burgalimar was surrendered to him.[1]

After a long time a certain noble Moor of Córdoba named Ibn Harach [Kharaj?], on the order of the king of Baeza, prudently arranged that the castle of Salvatierra should be surrendered to our king. The Moors, however, who held the castle, had rebelled against the king of Baeza and refused to restore the castle to him. Therefore, once the said Moor had the castle, he handed it over to the friars of Calatrava and to our king's men who had been sent especially for this purpose.[2] Thus, after a little labor and in a short time, by the power and grace of Our Lord Jesus Christ, King Fernando, whose actions are directed by the Lord, acquired that famous castle, fortified by art and nature, which the most illustrious Alfonso [VIII], was unable in any way to obtain, even though after the glorious triumph [of Las Navas de Tolosa] he had recovered all the other castles that had been lost in that area at the time of the battle of Alarcos, and certain others that he recently acquired beyond the Puerto del Muradal.

After returning again to Castile, the lord king, through royal munificence, distributed stipends to his noble vassals. With not much of an army he left Toledo around the feast of Pentecost in the era 1264 [A.D. 1226], and at first with a few men besieged the noble, strong, and famous castle of Capilla.[3]

When the siege was established, as our king assaulted the castle with marvelous machines, the Moors of Córdoba, who neither fear God nor revere man,[4] conspired in the customary manner to kill their king and lord, namely, the king of Baeza. When the king discovered this, he fled with a few people, but the Cordo-

---

[1] Fernando III was in Toledo by 8 January 1226.

[2] Salvatierra had been the seat of the Order of Calatrava after the loss of Calatrava itself following the battle of Alarcos. The crusaders en route to Las Navas de Tolosa had bypassed Salvatierra.

[3] By April 1226 Fernando III had returned to Toledo from Burgos. Pentecost Sunday fell on 7 June. See chap. 18 on stipends.

[4] Luke 18:4: "While it is true that I [a judge] neither fear God nor respect any human being. . . ."

bans followed and caught up with him at the castle of Almodóvar where they beheaded him. They sent his head to the king of Morocco, his mortal enemy, who, not many days before, had crossed over from Seville into the land of Morocco. As many have said, he struck what was offered to him with a rod that he had in his hand, and uttered insolent words to his [the king of Baeza's] dishonor and that of his whole family. When a certain brother of the king of Baeza responded to him sharply, he was struck by the king of Morocco himself with a sword, and thus, sedition broke out, and many from both sides died in mutual slaughter. This we learned from reports spread about.[5]

---

[5] Al-Bayâsî, who had been defeated near Seville by the governor, Abû-l-'Ulâ, had returned to Córdoba; he was killed at Almodóvar del Río about fifteen miles west of Córdoba in the summer of 1226. Abû-l-'Ulâ sent his head to his brother, the caliph al-'Âdil who crossed into Morocco after the murder of the caliph 'Abd al-Wâhid in September. The Castilians who held the alcázar of Baeza now occupied the entire town. See Lomax, The Reconquest of Spain, 139; O'Callaghan, Medieval Spain, 338.

50. THE FALL OF CAPILLA. UNSUCCESSFUL CAMPAIGNS OF THE KINGS OF PORTUGAL AND LEÓN

Our king, manfully intent on what he had undertaken, tirelessly by day and night and without letup attacked the castle that he had besieged in every way possible, although it seemed impregnable to some. After hearing of the king of Baeza's death, they advised the king to abandon the siege and move on to the region of Córdoba, where he would be able to inflict much damage on the Moors, and especially on the people of Córdoba, for killing his noble vassal, the king of Baeza. The king himself, however, following the counsel of his prudent mother, who had advised him not to withdraw from the siege for any reason until he had taken the castle, remained firm and constant in that intention, and did not give the besieged Moors any rest by day or by night.

Seeing the king's determination and constancy, the Moors, worn out by daily labor and the long wait, made a pact with him, and gave hostages: that if the king of Seville, who was then at Córdoba, would help them within eight days, so that they forced our king to withdraw from the siege, they would receive their hostages safely without any harm or injury; otherwise, they would surrender the castle to our king, saving their persons and whatever movable goods they could carry. After sending envoys to the king of Seville who received them, they were certain that that king would not come to their aid — for it was abhorrent for a king of mature age to fight against a spirited youth resolute in his purpose — they surrendered the castle of Capilla to our lord the king, to the honor and glory of Our Lord Jesus Christ.[1]

Now the king, keeping faith even with enemies, had the Moors and their wives and children and their movable goods taken safely, as he had promised, to the castle called Gahet. Then, by the power of Our Lord Jesus Christ and his most victorious cross, the archbishop of Toledo, the bishop of Palencia,[2] and other religious men who were with the bishops, cleansed the mosque of the Moors of all the filthiness of Muhammadan superstition, and dedicated it as a church to the

---

[1] Abû-l-'Ulâ was the governor of Seville. The siege lasted from 7 June to 15 August 1226.

[2] Archbishop Rodrigo of Toledo and Tello, bishop of Palencia (1217–1246). The castle of Gahet or Belalcázar was about twenty-five miles southwest of Almadén and about forty miles northwest of Córdoba. See Lomax, *The Reconquest of Spain,* 139.

Lord Jesus Christ, celebrating mass and the divine offices with great joy.[3]

The king, meantime, after repairing the wreckage and breaks in the walls, as the opportunity allowed, and providing the castle with food, arms, machines of war, and warlike men, returned to Toledo to his mother around the feast of the Assumption of Blessed Mary [15 August] with great joy and honor.

During that same summer the king of León besieged Badajoz and the king of Portugal besieged Elvas near Badajoz. As their hope was frustrated after a long siege, they withdrew from the besieged towns and each one returned to his own land. It is not ours to say what those kings and their vassals may have done, and how they may have conducted themselves in such a noble affair that they had undertaken by virtue of a joint agreement concluded between them many days before; different people think different things, but the opinion of one and all is that, after innumerable expenses and the deaths of men, the Saracens glory in the defense of those towns and retain them even now. It is said, moreover, by many worthy of belief that the king of Portugal, abandoned by his own men, withdrew, moaning and sorrowing beyond what is believable. The king of León, however, unwilling to endure the heat of summer, turned his face toward Galicia, planning to visit the tomb of the Blessed Apostle James.[4]

---

[3] While the choir chanted the antiphon *Asperges me* [derived from Psalms 51(50):9: "Cleanse me with hyssop, that I may be pure; wash me, make me whiter than snow"], the mosque (*mezquita*) was probably purified by the sprinkling of holy water and salt, and the walls were washed. An altar was erected and mass dedicating the church in honor of one of the saints was then celebrated.

[4] Badajoz lies on the Guadiana river (the effective border between León and Portugal), about twelve miles east of Elvas. The campaign by Sancho II of Portugal (1223–1248) and Alfonso IX of León took place in June or early July 1226. Alfonso IX was in Santiago de Compostela on 11 January 1227. The author's comment that the Saracens retained both towns "even now" indicates that this section of the *Chronicle* was written before 1230 when Alfonso IX finally captured Badajoz. See introduction.

THE REIGN OF FERNANDO III

51. LOUIS VIII, KING OF FRANCE, ATTACKS THE ALBIGENSIAN HERETICS

In the year when our lord the king waged war against the Saracens and destroyed Quesada, Louis, king of the French, gathered a large and powerful army and descended into Poitou and took the noble castle of Niort and the town called Saint Jean d'Angely. Eventually he besieged the famous town of La Rochelle, which surrendered to him after a long siege. King Louis had succeeded to the kingdom of his father, King Philip, who had died in the era 1261 [A.D. 1223].[1]

In that summer when our lord the king besieged and, through the power of our Lord Jesus Christ, took the castle of Capilla, that same King Louis, on the counsel and authority of the legate of the Roman Church who then held the place of the pope in the land of the French, invaded the territory of Provence against the heretics and their defenders. Indeed he came with a strong hand and outstretched arm[2] with a great and very powerful army. With many machines of war he besieged the famous city of Avignon, which surrendered to the king and the legate after a long siege. After he had subjugated almost all the land except Toulouse and a few other castles, while he was returning to his own land he died in Auvergne. Many great men and nobles, many men of middle status, and many people of low rank died in that siege.[3]

---

[1] The three towns supported Henry III of England (1216–1272) and so were taken in 1224 by Louis VIII (1223–1226), the son of Philip II Augustus. See Hallam, *Capetian France,* 187–188.

[2] Deuteronomy 5:15: "The Lord, your God, brought you from there [Egypt] with his strong hand and outstretched arm."

[3] Louis VIII and the legate, Cardinal Romanus, led a crusade against the Albigensian heretics. Avignon was taken on 9 September 1226 after a siege of three months. Louis VIII then died on 8 November 1226. See Hallam, *Capetian France,* 189–190.

52. THE SUBMISSION OF THE COUNT OF TOULOUSE
TO LOUIS IX AND BLANCHE OF CASTILE

When the count of Toulouse and his supporters heard of the death of Lord Louis, the illustrious king of the French, they were filled with very great joy. They prepared to rebel against the church and the French people, hoping that the youth of the king and the female sex would not be able to undertake anything important. For Louis, a tender boy of about twelve years of age, the son of King Louis, succeeded him, and his mother, Queen Lady Blanche, the daughter of the glorious King Lord Alfonso of Castile, assumed the care of the boy and the kingdom, and like a prudent woman, held the kingdom of the French and ruled it for a long time.[1]

After diligent discussion with the legate of the Roman Church who was then in France, and with the archbishops, bishops, and other prelates of the churches and with the barons of the realm, they dispatched noble men, brave and prudent, with a great array of knights and sergeants against the count of Toulouse and his supporters. Like knights of Christ and unconquered warriors, they gave no rest to the Toulousains and subjected the whole of that land, destitute of God's help, to the Roman Church, through the mediation of the king of the French.

Now the count of Toulouse, seeing that he could not rebel, submitted himself to the will of the legate and the king of the French, and was reconciled to the church in France, after first receiving from him [the legate] a sufficient punishment: that is, after swearing an oath that he would abide by the commands of the church in all things and would not leave France before he had fulfilled all the conditions that could then be fulfilled. The count's only daughter, whose marriage to a brother of the king of France was discussed, was taken to the queen of France, her cousin, as the count prolonged his stay in France.[2]

---

[1] Count Raymond VII of Toulouse saw Louis VIII's intervention as an effort to establish royal control in Languedoc. Louis IX (1226–1270) was the son of Louis VIII and Blanche of Castile, the daughter of Alfonso VIII. See Riley–Smith, *The Crusades*, 138–139; Hallam, *Capetian France,* 133–134.

[2] Raymond VII had been excommunicated by the Council of Bourges in 1225. By the terms of the treaty of Paris (12 April 1229) his daughter and principal heir, Jeanne, was betrothed to Alphonse of Poitiers, the king's brother. After Count Raymond's death in 1249, Alphonse took possession of the county in his wife's name. Jeanne and Blanche of Castile were great-granddaughters of Alfonso VII of León–Castile. Our author distinguishes between France and Languedoc, because the French kings did not yet have direct control over the latter area.

In the year from the Incarnation of the Lord 1229[3] the walls of Toulouse were entirely destroyed; the moats were made fully level to the surface of the land; and all the fortresses round about were destroyed, except a few which the king of the French retained in his hand. Thus Christ the Lord, our Savior, destroyed all the defenses raised up against Him. The heretical depravity that had almost established its nest in that land was destroyed in great part; many heretics were given over to fire and others fled or were dispersed. The Most High provided for their dispersion lest they should be the occasion of the subversion of many. That land was quiet therefore,[4] and peace, which had been lacking for some time, was restored to it.

---

[3] This is the first occasion on which the author dates an event, not according to the Spanish era, but rather according to that of the Incarnation of Jesus Christ.

[4] Psalms 76(75):9: "The earth feared and was silent"; 1 Maccabees 1:3: "The earth fell silent before him" (quoted above, chap. 5, n. 5 and chap. 26, n. 8).

53. THE REBELLION OF IBN HÛD OF MURCIA
AGAINST THE ALMOHADS

After the capture of the castle of Capilla, the king of Seville, who then presented himself as Miramamolín,[1] began to talk about a truce with our lord the king, promising a lot of money, part of which he paid; he was bound to pay the remaining part at a future time.

Now at that time a certain plebeian *almogávar*, courageous in war, as they said, by the name of Ibn Hûd, rebelled in the kingdom of Murcia and fought against the Murcians;[2] after conquering them, he captured their king and placed him in chains, and seized the city and the kingdom, following the counsel of a certain [. . .],[3] a powerful and prudent Moor, whom Ibn Hûd himself killed afterward.

With an inexorable hatred he persecuted the Almohads, publicly preaching that one should not obey them, because they were schismatics in their law, for they did not obey the lord of Baghdad, who is of the family of Muhammad.[4] For that reason he said their mosques should be cleansed because they were polluted by the Almohad superstition. He said that the Almohads themselves were oppressors of the people and violent extortioners; he also said that he was the liberator of the people of Andalucía. For thus the land of the Moors on this side of the sea is called, whence the people are called Andalusians, whom some believe to be the Vandals.[5]

---

[1] On the assassination of his brother al-'Âdil in 1227, Abû-l-'Ulâ, the governor of Seville, proclaimed himself as caliph, taking the honorific name al-Ma'mûn; he ruled until 1232.

[2] The term *almogávar* meant a lightly armed soldier, usually a foot soldier. Ibn Hûd (1228–1238), who belonged to the family of the twelfth-century kings of Zaragoza, was proclaimed in Murcia on 5 August 1228. Lomax, *The Reconquest of Spain*, 139–141, described Ibn Hûd as a "soldier of the regular army"; cf. O'Callaghan, *Medieval Spain*, 339.

[3] Charlo Brea, in his first translation, *Crónica*, 75, noted the lacuna, translating "de cierto . . . moro poderoso." In his second translation, *Crónica*, 84, he omitted this lacuna, translating "de cierto moro poderoso."

[4] In opposition to the Almohad caliphs of Morocco, Ibn Hûd recognized the Abbâsid caliph of Baghdad as the true successor of Muhammad.

[5] The Vandals, a Germanic tribe, invaded Spain in the fifth century and occupied the southernmost province of Baetica, now called Andalucía. In 429 they crossed into Mauretania (later Morocco), where their kingdom was conquered by the Byzantine emperor Justinian in 534. The name Andalucía probably derives from the Atlantic Ocean rather than from the Vandals. See Joaquín Vallvé, "Sobre algunas problemas de la invasión musulmana," *Anuario de Estudios Medievales* 4 (1967): 361–367.

Now the Andalusians, believing that divine power was at work within him —
because it is the custom of that people to follow new things with easy persuasion
— abandoned the lord of the Almohads and followed Ibn Hûd as king and lord.
In order to please them and to solidify the mortal enmity between the Almohads
and the Andalusians, he viciously fell upon the Almohads, decapitating men,
strangling them, inflicting diverse punishments on them, cutting off the breasts of
women, and extinguishing the life of children by a miserable death.

When the king of Seville heard that Murcia, together with Ibn Hûd, had rebelled against him, he gathered an army and advanced to that region and besieged
Murcia, but his plan was frustrated and he returned to the city of Seville.[6] Although the Murcians sustained much damage during the siege, they adhered firmly
nevertheless to Ibn Hûd; by their counsel and aid Ibn Hûd acquired almost all of
Andalucía within a short time. Indeed, the Andalusians spontaneously submitted
to him, withdrawing themselves from the dominion of the Almohads which
seemed heavy and intolerable to them.

Realizing that he was in imminent danger, the king of Seville left his son in
his place at Seville, and went to Ceuta; he pretended that the reason for his withdrawal was that he wanted to go oversea to seek help against those who were rebelling. The people of Seville, however, took his son and put him in chains, and
indicated to Ibn Hûd that he should come as king to receive their service and
obedience. He sent his brother to them, whom they received honorably in his
stead.[7]

The people of Granada, Jaén, Córdoba, and all the other surrounding towns
received Ibn Hûd as lord and king. The Almohads, moreover, who held the fortress of Jaén, surrendered to him, saving their lives and those of their children and
wives. A grandson of King Lope rebelled against the king of Valencia, who belonged to the Almohad family. Seeing this, the king of Valencia came over to our
lord, the king of Castile, begging his help against the rebels. Thus in a short time
Ibn Hûd held almost all of Andalucía except Valencia, in which the Moor mentioned above rebelled.[8]

---

[6] The city of Murcia, the seat of the old *taifa* of Murcia, lies about 270 miles east of
Seville.

[7] Abû-l-'Ulâ, the governor of Seville, who had proclaimed himself as caliph, crossed
the Strait of Gibraltar to Ceuta and entered the Almohad capital of Marrakech in late November 1228. The people of Seville submitted to Ibn Hûd in October 1229.

[8] Zayyân ibn Mardânish, a grandson of Lope ibn Mardânish, who had opposed the Almohads in the late twelfth century, overthrew Abû Zayd, the king of Valencia, in 1229.

54. THE MISSION OF CARDINAL JEAN D'ABBEVILLE, 1228–1229

Now the cunning and astute king of Valencia, sensing that the people subject to him were preparing to rebel, given that there was so much dissension in the entire kingdom of Morocco oversea, secretly notified the Lord Pope, Gregory IX, that he wished to become a Christian and to subject his kingdom to the Church of Rome.[1] He begged him to send a legate, a prudent, discreet, and learned man, for this purpose. That was the chief reason why the pope sent to Spain as legate, the prudent, discreet, and learned Master Jean d'Abbeville, bishop of Santa Sabina, as he told us personally.

Thus the legate entered Spain around the feast of the Assumption [15 August], in the year of the Incarnation of the Lord 1228. Traversing the provinces, he convoked synods, establishing certain new things according to the wisdom given him by God, to the honor of God and the honor of the clergy and the government of the churches. But when he decreed certain things against concubinary clergy and their children born of concubines, so much conflict broke out between the bishops and the clergy that had not been seen since times past.[2]

As the legate hoped for and expected the conversion of the king of Valencia, envoys were sent back and forth between the king and the legate. The king, expelled from his kingdom, as we touched on above, came to our lord the king and had a meeting with the legate in our kingdom.

Frustrated by the hope he had conceived of the conversion of the king, the lord legate, after the feast of Easter in the year of the Incarnation of the Lord 1229, rendered at Tarazona a sentence of divorce between the king of Aragón, Lord Jaime, and Queen Lady Leonor, because of notorious incest, for they were related to one another in the third degree of kindred.[3]

---

[1] Abû Zayd, the dispossessed king of Valencia, appealed to Pope Gregory IX (1227–1241) for help, and eventually converted to Christianity, taking the name of Vincent.

[2] The legate convoked synods in the ecclesiastical provinces of Compostela, Braga, Tarragona, and Toledo. See Peter Linehan, *The Spanish Church and the Papacy in the Thirteenth Century* (Cambridge: Cambridge University Press, 1971), 20–34.

[3] The legate held a council at Tarazona in April 1229, and pronounced against the marriage of Jaime I, king of Aragón (1213–1276), and Leonor, the daughter of Alfonso VIII, though he legitimated their son Alfonso. Jaime and Leonor were both great-grandchildren of Alfonso VII of León–Castile. See Robert I. Burns, S.J., "The Spiritual Life of James the Conqueror, King of Arago–Catalonia, 1208–1276: Portrait and Self Portrait," *Catholic Historical Review* 62 (1976): 1–35.

During that same time the king of León seized the famous castle of Cáceres. The legate, having executed his office, and having finished his legation, at the end of the month of August left Castile to return to Rome whence he had come.[4]

---

[4] Alfonso IX captured Cáceres, a key to further Leonese expansion to the south, on 23 April 1229. The legate left Spain for Rome in August 1229.

55. JAIME I OF ARAGÓN AND
THE CONQUEST OF MALLORCA, 1229

Now the king of Aragón, desirous of consecrating the first deeds of his youth to the Lord, assembled in Catalonia an army of nobles, people, and some prelates of churches. Around the feast of the Nativity of Blessed Mary [8 September 1229] he set sail for the island called Mallorca. Disembarking from their ships, they were opposed by the Moors of Mallorca with whom they engaged; by divine power the Moors yielded that first day to the Christians.[1]

On the following day, when Guillem de Montcada, a brave and prudent man, and his troops preceded the king of Aragón toward [the city of] Mallorca, they fell into an ambush of the Moors, and there he was killed and many nobles of Catalonia with him.[2] Although they followed afar off, when the king and those who were with him heard the clash of arms and the tumult of the combatants,[3] they came up hastily to the place; finding that nobleman and many others dead, they engaged the Moors and, with the help of God, killed many of them, while others fled and shut themselves up in the city of Mallorca.

A siege was established, and after innumerable efforts and intolerable sufferings because of the lack of food and the harshness of winter, which was more difficult than usual, they captured the city and the king himself and the king of Almería, who had come there by chance, together with all their people; many thousands of Moors were killed in the capture [of the city].[4] Praise be to God on high to whom it is equally easy to conquer a few or many![5]

As we know from the letters of the illustrious king,[6] when the city[7] was taken

---

[1] The crusading fleet of about 150 ships set sail on 5 September and landed on the night of 8–9 September. See Lomax, *The Reconquest of Spain,* 141–142; Bisson, *The Medieval Crown of Aragon,* 63–65; O'Callaghan, *Medieval Spain,* 340–343.

[2] Guillem de Montcada, viscount of Béarn, belonged to one of the great Catalan noble houses. He was killed in the battle of Portopí.

[3] Perhaps an allusion to Job 39:25: "Even from afar he scents the battle, the roar of the chiefs and the shouting."

[4] The city of Mallorca (modern Palma de Mallorca) was taken by assault on 31 December 1229. The king of Mallorca was Abû Yahyâ, and the king of Almería, Yahyâ al-Râmîmî.

[5] Again 1 Samuel (1 Kings) 14:6: "It is no more difficult for the Lord to grant victory through a few than through many" (quoted above, chap. 30, n. 11).

[6] This passage indicates that the author, as an official of Fernando III, had access to correspondence from King Jaime I.

there were with him scarcely 700 noble knights and 13,000 foot soldiers. The city was taken on the last day of the month of December in the year of the Incarnation of the Lord 1229. The king of Mallorca died within a few days after his son, whom he loved tenderly, was decapitated; and so it is believed that he died of extreme grief.

---

[7] Cirot and Cabanes Pecourt and Charlo Brea in his first edition of the *Crónica*, 79, omit *civitas*, the city.

56. ALFONSO IX OF LEÓN TRIUMPHS
OVER IBN HÛD AT ALANGE

Thus, except for a certain very strong castle, the whole island was subjected [. . .][1] to the king, to the honor and glory of our Lord Jesus Christ.

Around the beginning of Lent, the king of León, with a small party of his knights and with certain towns entered the land of the Moors and besieged Mérida, a famous old city that was reduced at that time to the status of a small town; a metropolitan city, its dignity had been transferred to the church of Compostela. Wherefore the bishops belonging to the province of Lusitania, who anciently were subject to the archbishop of Mérida, were then subject to the archbishop of Compostela.[2]

Now while the king was occupied with the siege, certain friars of the Knighthood of Santiago, with a few others, seized the castle of Montánchez. The city of Mérida also surrendered to the king.[3]

Ibn Hûd, then busy in the region of Córdoba, gathered a multitude of knights and foot soldiers with the intention of fighting, and came to a certain castle near Mérida. When the king of León heard that Ibn Hûd was coming to fight against him, he marched away from Mérida and encamped beyond the river Guadiana. On the following morning both armies advanced to the field. Although those who were with the king of León were few in comparison to the host of Moors, they triumphed over them with the help of our Lord Jesus Christ. Many of them were killed and Ibn Hûd himself fled and escaped in confusion.[4]

---

[1] The rest of the line is blank in the manuscript, but it may be that no words are missing.

[2] Ash Wednesday was 20 February 1230. In the ecclesiastical division of Spain in Roman and Visigothic times there were five provinces, each presided over by a metropolitan bishop (the archbishop of later times): Baetica (the metropolis of which was Seville), Lusitania (Mérida), Gallaetia (Braga), Tarraconensis (Tarragona), and Cartaginensis (Toledo). In 1120 Pope Calixtus II transferred the metropolitan rights of Mérida (then under Muslim rule) to the bishop of Santiago de Compostela; four years later he made the transfer good for all time. Thus Santiago became an archiepiscopal see, and Mérida, after its conquest, had to be content with a bishop.

[3] Montánchez is about twenty miles south of Cáceres and the same distance north of Mérida. Mérida did not surrender until after the battle of Alange described in the next paragraph.

[4] The battle was fought at Alange, about ten miles southeast of Mérida. As a consequence of the Christian victory Mérida surrendered in March 1230.

57. THE OCCUPATION OF ELVAS BY THE PORTUGUESE

The inhabitants of Elvas, hearing that Ibn Hûd and those who were with him had been defeated in battle, abandoned that castle and fled by night. Certain Portuguese friars returning from the battle, where they were with the king of León, discovered that the gates of the town were open. They entered, and, finding no one, they seized the castle and informed the king of Portugal. When he heard that, he sent his knights and other armed men to hold the castle; thus that castle, famous in the region, was acquired by the grace of the Savior for the Christian name.[1]

---

[1] Elvas, on the border between Portugal and Spain, about ten miles west of Badajoz, surrendered on 26 May 1230. Sancho II (1223–1248) was the king of Portugal at the time. See Lomax, *The Reconquest of Spain,* 142.

58. THE CRUSADE OF EMPEROR FREDERICK II
TO THE HOLY LAND, 1228

At the same time that these things were happening, that is, in the year of the Incarnation of the Lord 1228, Frederick, emperor of the Romans, the son of the Emperor Henry, the son of the Emperor Frederick I, who had worn the cross for a long time, but did not follow Jesus, indeed did not wish to fulfill the vow that he had taken when he took the cross and sought frivolous reasons to remain in Sicily and Apulia which he ruled as king,[1] was excommunicated at last by the Lord Pope Gregory IX. Coerced and resisting, without obtaining absolution nor even, as was proper, asking for it, he set sail around the feast of the Exaltation of the Holy Cross [14 September] with a few knights and arrived in the Holy Land.[2] He ruled there as king, by reason of the child that he had by the daughter of King John of Jerusalem, to whom the kingdom belonged by hereditary right from her mother.[3] He remained in that land for the whole winter, doing nothing very great as befits imperial majesty; but trusting in his astuteness, he treated with the sultan of Babylon through his envoys, so that the sultan would relinquish to the emperor, as a friend rather than as an enemy, the city of Jerusalem, whose walls had been knocked down at the time that the Christians had captured Damietta.[4]

The sultan, however, retained the fortress of the Temple and power and jurisdiction over the Saracens living there; he left to the emperor, from whom he had

---

[1] Frederick II had been Roman emperor since 1220. See chap. 40.

[2] Frederick II took the crusaders' vow in 1215 and renewed it in 1223. Though he set sail on 8 September 1227, he fell ill and returned to port; consequently, Gregory IX excommunicated him in November; he then sailed off again in 1228 (see below). See Riley–Smith, *The Crusades*, 149–151; David Abulafia, *Frederick II. A Medieval Emperor* (Oxford: Oxford University Press, 1992), 164–201.

[3] In 1227 Frederick married Yolanda, the daughter of John of Brienne and Queen Maria of Jerusalem. Through his wife John claimed the title of king of Jerusalem, but on her death in 1213 the title passed to Yolanda. She gave birth to a son, Conrad, in 1228, but died soon afterwards. The kingdom thus belonged to Conrad, but Frederick in effect claimed it for himself. On John of Brienne see chap. 42.

[4] After being excommunicated by the pope, Frederick II, without seeking absolution, set out again for the Holy Land in June 1228. He negotiated with the sultan of Egypt, al-Kamil. The Fifth Crusade, in which John of Brienne took part, had captured Damietta at the mouth of the Nile in November 1220, but in the summer of 1221 the crusaders were forced to withdraw. See Riley–Smith, *The Crusades*, 145–149.

received many precious gifts, the rest of the city, which the Christians could not defend against the Moors whenever they wished to attack it.[5]

---

[5] Frederick II and the Sultan al-Kamil concluded a treaty on 18 February 1229; its terms were much as described by our author. See Riley–Smith, *The Crusades,* 151; Abulafia, *Frederick II,* 182–185.

59. THE PAPAL ARMY INVADES FREDERICK II'S TERRITORY IN APULIA

After concluding a treaty with the sultan for ten years under the most miserable and horrendous conditions, he withdrew his knights, crossbowmen, and arms from the land and returned to Apulia, prompted by the devastation wrought by a papal army in the kingdom of Apulia. King John, Count Thomas, and the legates of the Roman Church, namely, Master Pelagius of Spain, then bishop of Albano, formerly bishop-elect of León, and Lord John of Colonna, were in that army.[1]

At the time the emperor went oversea, he had appointed as his vicar in the kingdom of Apulia a certain duke, called the duke of Spoleto. On the emperor's command, as it was said, he assembled a multitude of Christians and Moors and invaded the Patrimony of Blessed Peter, ravaging the land, occupying castles, and atrociously killing many through the agency of the Moors. Thus he advanced almost as far as Perugia where the pope and the cardinals were residing at that time.[2]

Pope Gregory IX and those who were with him, lamenting and sorrowing over the wicked killing of Christians and the miserable devastation of the land, and also fearing for themselves and theirs, summoned King John, whom he had appointed as his vicar in his cities and castles. He also summoned to the aid of the Roman Church the Lombards, who belonged to the League of Milan, and dispatched his army against the duke. He [the duke of Spoleto] fled and was expelled from the Patrimony of Blessed Peter, and the papal army invaded Apulia, occupying certain cities and towns by force, while others spontaneously surrendered to the Lord Pope.[3]

About the beginning of June in the year of the Incarnation of the Lord 1229, the emperor returned to Apulia and remained there because he did not have a large enough army to resist or to attack the papal army. An astute man, he held out until the stipends given to the papal army began to run out. As the diminished

---

[1] Infuriated by Frederick's departure on crusade, Gregory IX sent an army, commanded by John of Brienne, the former king of Jerusalem, to invade Apulia. The other leaders were Count Thomas of Acerra, Pelagius, cardinal bishop of Albano, formerly legate during the Fifth Crusade, and John of Colonna, cardinal priest of St. Praxedis. See Joseph P. Donovan, *Pelagius and the Fifth Crusade* (Philadelphia: University of Pennsylvania Press, 1950).

[2] Frederick's vicar in Sicily, Duke Rainald of Spoleto, now appointed imperial vicar in the march of Ancona, invaded the papal states with an army that included Muslims.

[3] The pope appealed to the Lombard League on 26 June 1229.

army began to retreat, the emperor regained his strength and recovered certain castles and certain cities that he had lost, though the Lord Pope's men retained some. The emperor came to San Germano with his army and besieged the bishop of Albano in the castle of Monte Cassino. At last a truce, not for a long period, was agreed upon by the pope and the emperor. The bishop, bothered by a serious illness, returned to the curia and died, and was buried at Perugia at the feet of the Lord Pope Innocent III.[4]

The truce was prolonged, and peace and concord between the emperor and the church was discussed. By the grace of God, at the beginning of the month of September in the year 1230 the emperor came to Anagni, where the pope was, and at his feet they were reconciled. Peace was established under certain conditions that are too long to write here.[5]

---

[4] Frederick landed at Brindisi on 10 June 1229. Pelagius died at Monte Cassino on 30 June 1230.

[5] Papal representatives negotiated the peace of San Germano with Frederick in 1229, but the treaty was not signed until 23 July 1230. See Abulafia, *Frederick II*, 200–201.

60. THE DEATH OF ALFONSO IX OF LEÓN

In the same year, around the feast of the Nativity of St. John the Baptist [24 June], our King Lord Fernando besieged the strongly fortified city of Jaén, upon which he inflicted a great deal of damage. But at last, seeing that he was not succeeding, both because of the multitude of defenders within and because of the strength of the place, he abandoned the siege around the feast of St. Michael [29 September].[1]

Just a few days before the feast of St. Michael, Lord Alfonso, king of León, the father of our king, came to a happy end, as it is believed, and departed from this world at Villanueva near Sarria in Galicia. He ended his life zealous for justice, manfully and wisely pursuing thieves and other evildoers.[2]

When his daughters heard of their father's death, although they were not far away from the place where their father died, they quickly turned about and went to Astorga, but they were not received as they wished. In indignation they left there and went to León, where they also were not received as they wished. For the response of the people and of the bishops was that they would receive and willingly serve those persons [the king's daughters], but they would not admit their knights and armed men. They went to Benavente where they received a similar response. Finally they went to Zamora with their mother Queen Lady Teresa, who always accompanied them.[3] There they were admitted, because Rodrigo Fernández, nicknamed el feo (the ugly one), the son of Count Froilán, and many others favored those noble ladies.[4]

Now our king heard of the death of his father before he entered Toledo where his mother and his wife were. After taking counsel with his mother, the archbishop, and the magnates who were there at the time, he rapidly crossed the mountains, and making his way by Ávila, came to Medina. Then certain people from Toro and from some other towns of the kingdom of León came to him and

---

[1] See Lomax, *The Reconquest of Spain,* 142.

[2] Alfonso IX died on 24 September 1230. Villanueva de Sarria is about fifty miles southeast of Santiago de Compostela.

[3] By his second wife, Teresa of Portugal, Alfonso IX had two daughters, Sancha and Dulce. Their journey took them eastward to Astorga, about forty miles west of León; from León, they headed south about forty-five miles to Benavente, and from there, forty miles farther south to Zamora.

[4] Rodrigo Fernández, the son of Fernán Rodríguez de Cabrera, married the daughter of Count Froila (or Froilán) Vermúdez de Trastámara.

found him at Medina. The king himself rejected certain foolish ideas that were suggested to him; he crossed the Duero and came to Villalar, and the people of that town immediately admitted him. On the following day he went to San Cebrián de Mazote, where he was likewise admitted. On the next day, that is, the feast of St. Luke [18 October 1230], he was admitted into Toro and they did homage to him. Leaving there after three days he came to Villalpando, held by Queen Lady Berenguela; from there he went to Mayorga where he was received with great joy and honor. Then passing through Mansilla he came to León. The bishop and clergy and all the inhabitants of the place who had suffered many injuries on his account [. . .].[5] However, García Rodríguez Carlota, the *merino mayor*, held the towers of the city.[6]

But when our king prolonged his stay in that city, refusing to leave until he first secured the towers, Queen Teresa and her daughters and supporters went to Villalobos and communicated with Queen Lady Berenguela, asking her to deign to come to Valencia. She also would come to her at that town. And so it was done.[7]

---

[5] A verb, presumably something like *received him*, is missing in the manuscript.

[6] From Toledo Fernando III moved about sixty miles northward to Ávila, then about sixty miles to Medina del Campo; from there he moved northwest crossing the Duero, passing through Villalar and San Cebrián de Mazote, to Toro, a distance of about twenty-five miles from Medina. Then he turned northward to Villalpando (part of Queen Berenguela's marriage settlement), about twenty miles from Toro; another twenty miles took him to Mayorga, another twenty to Mansilla, and about eight to León. The *merino mayor* was a royal provincial administrator.

[7] Presumably Queen Teresa came north from Zamora to Villalobos, just above Villalpando. Valencia [later Valencia de Don Juan] is about twenty miles south of León.

61. FERNANDO III BECOMES KING OF LEÓN

The queens discussed peace and concord between the king and his sisters in that town. Peace and concord was concluded between them at Benavente. Present in that town were the two queens, the king and his sisters, the archbishops of Toledo and Compostela, and many barons and townsmen.[1]

The form of the compact was this: the king assigned to his two sisters 30,000 *maravedís* to be collected annually in certain places for as long as they lived. Many additional conditions are contained in the charters drawn up concerning this. The sisters renounced their rights to the kingdom, if they had any, and their father's charters given to them concerning the succession and donation of the kingdom were destroyed.[2] Furthermore, they ordered that whatever castles and fortresses were held by their people in their name should be handed over to our king, except some castles which certain trustees would hold to guarantee the compact.

With these things taken care of in this way, our king went to Zamora and was received honorably. Then he entered Extremadura where he was received by everyone with joy and honor. Thus in a short time, with the help of God, in whose hand is the kingdom of men,[3] our king held his father's kingdom in peace, except Galicia. He was unable immediately to go there where no small disturbance had been going on from the time of his father's death. Thus the two kingdoms, which had been separated on the death of the emperor, were united in the person of our king.[4]

---

[1] Benavente is about twenty miles south of Valencia and forty-five miles south of León. The archbishops were Rodrigo Jiménez de Rada of Toledo and Bernardo of Santiago de Compostela.

[2] The pact was concluded at Benavente on 11 December 1230. For the text see González, *Fernando III*, 2:311–314, no. 270. *Maravedís* were gold coins.

[3] Cf. Daniel 4:14, 4:29, 5:21 (quoted above, chap. 14, n. 9).

[4] Fernando III's journey to Zamora, Salamanca, and other towns in Leonese Extremadura took place in January–March 1231. Alfonso VII had divided Castile and León between his two sons in 1157.

62. FERNANDO III PACIFIES GALICIA AND ASTURIAS

In the following year, around the Nativity of the Lord, the king entered Galicia and brought peace where there had been disorder. After correcting many injuries, by means of a true inquest, and after promulgating certain constitutions against turbulent people and evildoers in that land, he went to Oviedo in Asturias where he stayed for a short time. Amending injuries and pacifying the land, he left there and passed through León and went to Carrión, where his mother met him. His wife had remained there for a long time. Many people from the kingdom of León and many nobles from Galicia and Asturias gathered with him there; some of them he sent away, and others he took with him to Burgos.[1]

---

[1] Fernando III visited Galicia from late December 1231 to May 1232. He was in Oviedo on 3 June; in León on 15 June; Carrión on 25 June; and Burgos on 11 July 1232. In a "true inquest" ["per inquisicionem ueram"] local people were put on oath to identify lawbreakers.

LATIN CHRONICLE OF THE KINGS OF CASTILE

63. FERNANDO III CONDUCTS BUSINESS IN BURGOS

A great multitude of people, commoners and nobles both from Castile and Galicia and other parts of the kingdom, came to that city where the king remained for a long time, expediting many kinds of business with the counsel of good men.[1]

---

[1] The king was in Burgos at least from 11–30 July 1232.

64. THE FALL OF ÚBEDA, BORRIANA, AND TRUJILLO, 1233

In the following winter in the era 1271 [A.D. 1233], on the feast of the Epiphany [6 January], the lord king besieged Úbeda[1] with his nobles and a few people from the kingdom of León, as well as the people of Toro, Zamora, Salamanca, and Ledesma, who, in obedience to the king's orders, hastened to the siege of the town in a great host and with a lot of equipment. As the time approached up to which they were bound to serve the king according to their *fuero*, as they said, they returned home before the capture of the town. But the king persevered in the siege with the Castilians and the nobles of the kingdom of León until, by the grace of Jesus Christ, that famous town, so often mentioned, once endowed with riches and a host of people, was delivered into his hands in the month of July. Indeed neither Ibn Hûd nor any other powerful Moors from this side of the sea dared to come to the relief of the town.[2]

Those who were besieged in the fortress struggled under a shortage of bread and other victuals. On the condition that, saving the persons of the people of both sexes and the goods that they could carry, they would be permitted to leave, they yielded the fortress to the lord king. They withdrew after he gave them safe conduct to whatever place they chose.[3]

At the same time Lord Jaime, king of Aragón, besieged and captured the town of Borriana on the way toward the famous city of Valencia.[4] In the same winter

---

[1] Úbeda, one of the keys to control of the Upper Guadalquivir river, is located about seventy-five miles east of Córdoba and forty-five miles north of Granada. The siege lasted from 6 January to sometime in July 1233. At this point the author reverts to the use of the Spanish era instead of the year of the Incarnation.

[2] All these towns are in Leonese Extremadura: Toro is about twenty miles east of Zamora, which is about forty-five miles north of Salamanca; Ledesma is about twenty miles northwest of Salamanca. Their *fueros* or municipal charters limited their term of military service to the king to three months. Three months from the beginning of the siege on 6 January would be 6 April. Úbeda surrendered three months later, in July 1233. See James F. Powers, *A Society Organized for War. The Iberian Municipal Militias in the Central Middle Ages, 1000–1284* (Berkeley: University of California Press, 1988), 59.

[3] See Lomax, *The Reconquest of Spain*, 143.

[4] In December 1232 Jaime I took the crusader's vow. After a two-month siege, on 28 July 1233, he captured Borriana, on the Mediterranean coast about ten miles south of Castellón de la Plana and about thirty miles north of Valencia. See Lomax, *The Reconquest of Spain*, 147–148.

when our King Lord Fernando besieged Úbeda, the Master of Calatrava and the people of Plasencia together with their bishop besieged and captured the fortress of Trujillo.[5]

---

[5] Trujillo, about forty miles south of Plasencia (about one hundred and ten miles west of Toledo), was taken on the feast of the conversion of St. Paul, 25 January 1232. The Master of the Military Order of Calatrava was Gonzalo Yáñez.

65. THE REVOLT OF LOPE DÍAZ DE HARO
AND ALVAR PÉREZ

After the seizure of that noble town, the king returned to Castile and was received in Burgos with great joy and honor. He remained there for some time while he treated of great affairs touching the utility of the whole realm.[1]

He is believed to have offended Lope Díaz, one of the magnates of Castile.[2] The rancor, previously conceived during the siege of Úbeda, began to increase day by day, but the smoldering fire had not yet burst into flame. Then Lope Díaz, full of anger and indignation, withdrew from the king, especially, as he said, because he thought, by many signs, that he was held in disdain and contempt in the eyes of the king. Preparing to avenge himself, he began to discuss the concubinage of one of his daughters with Nunyo, count of Rousillon, the grandson of the count of Barcelona and Count Nuño of Castile; this took place after Easter in the year of grace 1234.[3]

Around that same Easter he arranged a similar concubinage, because the three were respectively related in the same degree, of his older daughter with Álvar Pérez; but this concubinage was consummated after the feast of St. Michael following.[4] The king and his mother the queen were in Burgos with the archbishop

---

[1] Fernando III was in Burgos in October–November 1233. The phrase "touching the utility of the whole realm" ["que tocius terre continebant utilitatem"] reflects the language of jurists influenced by Roman law when speaking of the affairs of kingdoms.

[2] Lope Díaz de Haro succeeded his father, Diego López, as the royal *alférez* or standardbearer (see chaps. 13, 15, 17, 22–24, 26–27 for Diego López). The cause of the conflict may have been the fact that Lope Díaz held seventeen castles in the king's name without having been formally invested with them by the royal *portero* or bailiff, as reported in chap. 66.

[3] Our author condemns this marriage as concubinage because the parties were related within the prohibited degrees of kindred. Lope Díaz arranged the marriage of his daughter Urraca to Count Nunyo of Rousillon, a grandson of Ramon Berenguer IV of Barcelona, and Count Nuño Pérez de Lara, and a great-grandson of Count Pedro González de Lara. Urraca was a great-great-granddaughter of Count Pedro. Count Nunyo was a third cousin of Lope Díaz, and a third cousin once removed of Urraca. See the genealogical chart in Cirot's edition, p. 138, n. 65.3. Easter fell on 23 April 1234. Here again the author reverts to the year of the Lord.

[4] Lope Díaz married his daughter Mencía to Álvar Pérez de Castro; she was a great-great-grandaughter of Rodrigo Fernández de Castro, and Álvar was a great-grandson. Thus Mencía and Álvar were third cousins once removed. See the genealogical chart in Cirot's edition, p. 139, n. 65.4. The feast of St. Michael was 29 September 1234.

of Toledo and the bishops of Burgos, Segovia, and Osma, namely the chancellor, by whom, on the counsel of the bishop of Astorga, who was then in the royal court, and other experts in law, Álvar Pérez and Mencía López, whom he had married, were solemnly and publicly excommunicated on Sunday in the church of Burgos, because of manifest incest contrary to the prior prohibition issued in Burgos by the archbishop of Toledo and the bishop of Burgos.[5]

On account of this concubinage quite a bit of disorder broke out in the kingdom, because the consent of the king, whose approval was necessary and expected as the uncle, that is, the brother of the girl's mother, and her protector because she was guarded in the chamber of Queen Lady Beatriz, was — I will not say disdained — not even requested.[6]

By means of this alliance, Álvar Pérez and Lope Díaz were bound together by a very firm bond, as they themselves admitted, against common enemies. The rest of the people suspected that the pact was directed against the familiars of the king — I will not say against the king. That appeared afterward. Indeed Álvar Pérez, insofar as he could, fortified with arms [. . .] and a moat the town of Paredes between Palencia and Carrión, which is his own inheritance. He said that he wanted to remain in his own estate and that, as he said, he was permitted to do so according to the *fuero* of Castile, although the king had already occupied the land that Álvar Pérez held from him.[7]

---

[5] Fernando III was in Burgos in October and November 1234. The prelates mentioned were Archbishop Rodrigo of Toledo; Bishops Mauricio of Burgos; Bernardo of Segovia; Juan of Osma, the chancellor, and the probable author of this chronicle (referring to himself in the third person); and Nuño of Astorga, who seems to have been a *jurisperitus* or expert in canon law who advised the others that the marriage was uncanonical.

[6] Fernando III was the uncle of Mencía and Urraca López because their mother Urraca Alfonso was an illegitimate daughter of Alfonso IX. Fernando III was a half-brother of Urraca Alfonso. Mencía was one of the ladies in Queen Beatriz's chamber.

[7] Paredes de Nava is about fifteen miles northeast of Palencia and the same distance southwest of Carrión. The *fuero* of Castile was the customary law regulating the affairs of nobles such as Álvar Pérez.

66. The End of the Revolt of Alvar Pérez
and Lope Díaz

When the king heard this, he was moved to anger, and, with the firm intention of attacking that town, he summoned the militia of his nobles and neighboring peoples. On that account he went to Palencia.[1] But Álvar Pérez, following wiser counsel, submitted himself to the will and disposition of the Queens, Lady Berenguela and Lady Beatriz. After taking counsel with prudent men, they ordered Álvar Pérez to leave Paredes as it was before and to go into exile from the whole kingdom to the land of the Saracens or elsewhere, there to remain until he was able to regain the king's grace; his supporters were restored to the king's favor. This was done under no condition and under no previous pact.

Lope Díaz recognized that the seventeen castles that he held in the kingdom of Castile, but had not received from the king's bailiff, belonged to the king. He received them from the king's hand, through his bailiff, and his land was assured to him for fifty years by Queen Lady Berenguela under many honorable conditions; her son confirmed his mother's decision. Thus through the grace of Him who is our peace,[2] all things were pacified and the land was quiet and calm.[3] These things were done in the town of Palenzuela around the feast of the Purification [2 February 1235].[4]

At the beginning of the following Lent, while the king was at Valladolid, Álvar Pérez, with his permission, directed his journey toward the land of the Saracens. But the queens, very prudent ladies, foreseeing the evils that might occur to our frontier from the alliance of Álvar Pérez and Ibn Hûd, the king of the Moors on this side of the sea, set to work efficaciously so that Álvar Pérez would be restored to the king's favor; that was done; and so he recovered his land and castles.[5]

---

[1] Fernando III was in Palencia in January 1235.

[2] Ephesians 2:14: "For he is our peace."

[3] Psalms 76(75):9: "The earth feared and was silent"; 1 Maccabees 1:3: "The earth fell silent before him" (quoted above, chap. 5, n. 5; chap. 26, n. 8; chap. 52, n. 4).

[4] Palenzuela lies on the Río Arlanza, about twenty-two miles southwest of Burgos.

[5] Ash Wednesday, the beginning of Lent, fell on 21 February 1235. Fernando III was in Valladolid at least on 29 January and 14 February 1235.

67. The Truce between Fernando III and Ibn Hûd

Later during the following spring, in the year of grace 1235, Álvar Pérez, on the king's command, went on ahead to the lands of the Saracens against Ibn Hûd. The king followed him with a noble militia and not many commoners. Then, after laying waste the harvests of Jaén and Arjona and the villages nearby, with Álvar Pérez as intermediary, he agreed with Ibn Hûd, who was then besieging Niebla between Seville and Portugal,[1] that Ibn Hûd, in return for a truce until the following May, would give our king 430,000 *maravedís*; about a third of that sum was paid immediately; another third was due to be paid at the end of the following September, and the final third at the end of January.[2]

With that settled, insofar as they were then able to confirm it, the king returned from the lands of Córdoba and besieged Iznatoraf, a very strong castle, which surrendered to him immediately, saving the persons of the Moors and the movable goods that they were able to carry. After entrusting the security[3] and the custody of the castle to a certain knight and to others with him, he went to the impregnable castle of San Esteban, which had caused much harm to the Christians, especially in blocking the roads going to Úbeda and Baeza. The *alcaide* of that place[4] and those who were with him surrendered the castle at once to the king, accepting from him a certain small sum of money and horses and I know not how many mules. After providing for those who would remain in the castle, the king returned to Toledo to his mother and wife.

Then, passing through Segovia on the vigil of the Assumption [14 August], he entered Burgos, where he was received with great joy and honor. It had been

---

[1] Jaén, one of the principal towns of Upper Andalucía, is about fifty miles east of Córdoba and about forty north of Granada. Arjona is about fifteen miles northwest of Jaén. Niebla is about thirty-five miles west of Seville.

[2] The truce may have been concluded in May 1235 to extend for another year. A third of the tribute (*parias*) was about 143,000 *maravedís*; the first third was paid immediately; the second was payable at the end of September 1235, and the final third at the end of January 1236.

[3] Cirot, Cabanes Pecourt, and Charlo Brea agree on the reading: "Circa igitur et custodia castri." In both his translations, but not in his edition, Charlo Brea indicates a lacuna following *circa*. Cirot cited Ducange's *Glossarium mediae et infimae latinitatis*, where *circa* is interpreted as *excubiae* or *vigilia*, meaning "watch" or "security".

[4] The *alcaide* was a castellan. Castellar de San Esteban or Santiestaban is about twenty miles northeast of Úbeda, and Iznatoraf is about twenty-five miles.

agreed when the truce was established that if the king wished to besiege or was able to capture the two castles mentioned above, Ibn Hûd would not defend them, and they were not included in the truce.[5]

---

[5] The king was in Segovia on 3 August and in Burgos from 13 August 1235. The castles of San Esteban and Iznatoraf were not included in the truce, so Ibn Hûd pledged not to defend them.

68. THE REVOLT OF THE ROMANS AGAINST POPE GREGORY IX

Near the same time, in the era mentioned, when a disturbance broke out in our realm, there was great discord between the Roman Church, then ruled by Gregory IX, and the Romans who were struggling to overthrow ecclesiastical liberty. They wished to impose an insupportable yoke with the most grave conditions on the cardinals and all the Roman clergy. The Romans also withdrew from the pope the rights which the pope had held from antiquity in the city, concerning both the coinage and the appointment of the senator [of Rome] and many other things. For that reason the pope and the cardinals went to Rieti and summoned Emperor Frederick from Apulia to them. After diligent discussion it was thus provided that the sentence of excommunication should be imposed on the senator and certain of the principal men of Rome.[1]

That sentence was immediately followed by the struggle[2] of the emperor against the senate and all the people of Rome. Consequently, the emperor, with the army that he had with him at that time, invaded the Roman territory doing a great deal of damage. After capturing certain castles that the Romans then held, he left a certain German count and a noble militia at Viterbo to defend the church. While the pope was then at Perugia, he [the emperor] returned to Apulia promising to return with a great and powerful army in the following summer. The Romans, taking this to heart, out of fear perhaps more than love, submitted their necks to the church and accepted all the apostolic mandates that had been in dispute. Security was given under oath by the senator and many of the nobles of Rome, and so peace was made between the church and the Romans.[3] Nevertheless, that security did not please certain cardinals who thought it was insufficient. Thus, as the peace was neither firm nor stable, neither the pope nor the cardinals wished to enter the city.

---

[1] The Romans forced Gregory IX to flee to Rieti in the summer of 1234. The Senator of Rome was Luca Savelli, who declared that the papal patrimony in Rome and Tuscany pertained to the commune of Rome. See also Abulafia, *Frederick II*, 237–238.

[2] *Dificatio*. Cirot, Cabanes Pecourt, and Charlo Brea agree on this reading. In his first translation of the *Crónica*, 91, Charlo Brea translated it as "la acción del emperador." In his second translation, *Crónica*, 96, he left *dificatio* untranslated and commented that he did not know the word or its juridical value. I suspect that *dificatio* is a copyist's error and that the word may have been *dimicatio*, "struggle" or "fight".

[3] After the peace of San Germano in 1230 (see chap. 59), Frederick II and Gregory IX generally acted in concert in Italy. The pope was in Perugia in September 1234–1235. A new Senator, Angelo Malabranca, made peace with the pope in May 1235.

Meantime the emperor, who had promised to return with an army to aid the church against the Romans, went to Germany[4] and took to wife the daughter of the king of England, who was then reigning, namely, King John, the son of Henry the Great, king of the English.[5] While the emperor remained in Germany he assembled a small army against the Lombards, that is, against Milan and its League, who were rebelling against him.[6] In the era 1274 [A.D. 1236], around the feast of St. Michael [29 September], he invaded Lombardy and inflicted much harm on the people of Mantua, and took Vicenza, part of which rebelled while another part favored him. Then the army rested during that winter. The emperor himself left the army in Lombardy and returned to Germany.[7]

At the same time the emperor of Constantinople, who was called Ianna, King John of Acre, the son-in-law of our Queen Lady Berenguela, was attacked by the Greeks and the city of Constantinople was almost put under siege. Therefore the emperor appealed to the Roman Church asking for help, but his plea was not heard as he wished.[8]

---

[4] Frederick II set out for Germany in April 1235, where he dethroned his son Henry, to whom he had entrusted the government, but who had rebelled against him. See Abulafia, *Frederick II*, 239–241.

[5] Then, on 15 July 1235, Frederick married Isabella, the sister of King Henry III of England (1216–1272). She was the daughter of King John (who had died in 1216 and obviously was not reigning at that time), son of Henry II, whom our author calls Henry the Great. See Abulafia, *Frederick II*, 242.

[6] The Lombard League was resistant to Frederick II's efforts to assert imperial authority over northern Italy. Gregory IX regarded the Lombards as allies. See Abulafia, *Frederick II*, 290–296.

[7] In this chapter the author again refers to the Spanish era. Frederick II burned Vicenza in November 1236. He returned to Germany to suppress the rebellion of the duke of Austria and to arrange the election of his son Conrad as king of the Romans. He returned to Lombardy in the fall of 1237 and inflicted a major defeat on the towns of the Lombard League at Cortenuova on 27 November, but that occurred after our author had concluded his *Chronicle*. See Abulafia, *Frederick II*, 296–301.

[8] See chap. 42. John of Brienne had married Berenguela, the daughter of Queen Berenguela. As Constantinople was threatened by Theodore, the despot of Epirus, and John Asen, the king of Bulgaria, the barons of the Latin Empire arranged the marriage of Emperor Baldwin II, then eleven years old, to Maria, the four-year-old daughter of John of Brienne and Berenguela. John was thus the effective emperor of Constantinople from 1231 to 1237 when he died. See Riley–Smith, *The Crusades,* 184–185; M. J. Angold, "John of Brienne," *ODB* 2:1062–1063.

69. THE CHRISTIANS BREAK INTO THE CITY OF CÓRDOBA

At the same time in the era written instead of that of Christ [. . .], namely, 1274 [A.D. 1236] while our lord King Fernando was at Benavente around the middle of January and his mother was staying at León,[1] he received envoys from those Christians who had secretly occupied a certain section of Córdoba at night. They implored him to help them because they were placed in most grave peril, for, with respect to the multitude of Córdoba, they were very few. They were separated from the Moors only by a certain wall running almost through the middle of the city. It was in the power of the Moors, whenever they wished, to leave the part of the city that they held to attack the Christians. In fact the Christians had fortified with arms and men certain very strong towers in the wall that they had occupied; other Christians fought against the Moors at the boundary between the part of the city that they held and the part that the Moors defended; many were killed on both sides.[2]

Indeed those Christians, as if inspired by the Holy Spirit, already knew about the situation of Córdoba: that few people lived in that part of the city that they had occupied. Pretending to go afar off, they came at night under the command of a certain person who had become a Christian after being a Moor, and who fully knew the situation of Córdoba, and scaled the wall with ladders; killing the sentries on the walls, they occupied that part of the city. They killed many of the inhabitants of that sector, while other inhabitants fled to the other part of the city. Córdoba looked out at a people of another religion and language,[3] whom she had not nourished, killing her sons and daughters as if in her bosom.[4] Stupefied, she was unable to strengthen dissolute hands and weak knees against the enemy; even though she saw them to be few, nevertheless she could not resist them, because the indignation of the Lord Jesus Christ and his power oppressed such a great and powerful multitude of Moors.

---

[1] Fernando III was in Benavente, about forty-five miles south of León, on 15 January 1236.

[2] The Christians seem to have broken into the Ajarquía, the eastern sector of the city that was separated by a wall from the Almedina, the main part of the city, on the west.

[3] Cf. Baruch 4:15: "He has brought against them a nation from afar, a nation ruthless and of alien speech."

[4] The language is reminiscent of 1 Kings 3:19–21 relating the judgment of Solomon in the dispute between two women, both of whom had given birth; one child died and both claimed the survivor.

The messengers mentioned above urged the lord king to aid his vassals who had exposed themselves to such a great danger in his service and for the honor of the Christian faith, and to boldly take in hand the hour that the Lord had favored and offered to him, and to show himself a man before all who listened.[5]

---

[5] See Lomax, *The Reconquest of Spain*, 144–147.

70. FERNANDO III HASTENS TO AID THE CHRISTIANS IN CÓRDOBA

The Spirit of the Lord inspired the king,[1] who placed his hope in the Lord Jesus Christ and closed his ears lest he hear the counsel of those who, like wizards,[2] tried by persuasive words to prevent such a noble deed. They alleged the harshness of the winter, drenched with more rain than customary; the dangers of the roads; the flooding of rivers; the few nobles who were then with him; the uncertain outcome of such a great danger; and (what was more to be feared than anything else) the innumerable multitude of people in Córdoba, who, from ancient times, surpassed in bravery and the exercise of arms the other Moors on this side of the sea. He would be engaging them in battle over their own persons and over such a noble city, in the land of their birth, for their wives and children and all the goods they possessed.

One could fear reasonably enough the coming of their king, namely, Ibn Hûd, with all his power and the gathering of all the people from the adjacent cities who thought of Córdoba as a most stalwart shield and bastion against the Christians. It seemed to the Moors on this side of the sea that this was their business, for, once Córdoba was taken, the other cities, weakened and feeble, would not be able to resist the most powerful king of Castile and León. But spurning all of these things and thinking them nothing, King Fernando, the most brave knight of Christ, left Benavente on the following morning in great haste; from afar he greeted his mother (who was then at León) by a messenger, who was sent to announce to her faithfully what had happened and her son's firm intention that he was unable to change for any reason.

Making his way through Zamora, the king spoke briefly to the people, and, like an eagle swooping down on its prey,[3] he came to Salamanca; after stopping there for a short time, he gave whatever horses and arms he was able to obtain to the nobles who were with him. Insofar as was possible in such a short time, he readied those things that were necessary for such a journey and sent his chancellor,

---

[1] Again Judges 14:6: "But the Spirit of the Lord came upon Samson" (quoted above, chap. 18, n. 8; chap. 43, n. 2; chap. 48, n. 2).

[2] Psalms 58(57):5–6: "Their poison is . . . like that of a serpent stopping its ears, so as not to hear the voice of the charmer, who casts such cunning spells."

[3] Again Job 9:26: ". . . like an eagle swooping on its prey"; Ezekiel 22:25: "Her princes are like roaring lions that tear prey" (quoted above, chap. 12, n. 8 and chap. 44, n. 2).

namely the bishop of Osma,[4] to his mother to distribute stipends among the knights who said they would follow him. He took the most direct route, not turning to the right toward Ciudad Rodrigo, nor to the left toward Talavera and Toledo, both of which roads seemed easier; and so he came to Mérida.[5]

---

[4] Juan, bishop of Osma (1231–1240), was the royal chancellor from 1217 to 1246; the probable author of this *Chronicle*, he refers to himself in the third person.

[5] The king journeyed southward from Benavente: about thirty miles to Zamora, forty to Salamanca, and, then probably about forty to Béjar, thirty to Plasencia, forty to Cáceres, and forty to Mérida. Ciudad Rodrigo is about fifty miles southwest of Salamanca, and about another fifty to Plasencia. The distance from Salamanca to Talavera is about eighty miles; from there to Toledo is about forty-five miles.

71. FERNANDO III DIRECTS THE SIEGE OF CÓRDOBA

Then, not resting by day or night,[1] through impassable and deserted land, notwithstanding rivers that had overflowed and spilled over their banks, and muddy roads that impeded his journey, with a hostile sky above his head, almost entirely dissolved in rain, among the castles of the Moors, he achieved his wish, arriving at Córdoba on the seventh day of the month of February. O that happy day[2] on which the Christian people, who were then placed in such great danger in Córdoba, saw their king, who had exposed himself to so much danger so that he could succor his people!

The king found there with the people just mentioned Álvar Pérez, his noble and powerful vassal, and the bishop of Cuenca, who had come from the region of Toledo, after hearing that the Christians had seized part of Córdoba. The bishop of Baeza who was even closer came quickly with his people.[3] In the company of the lord king when he first came to Córdoba were fewer than a hundred noble knights; the magnates who had followed the king at that time and came to Córdoba with him were: his brother, Infante Lord Alfonso, Rodrigo Fernández, el feo (the ugly one), Gil Manrique, Álvar Fernández, Diego González, the son of Count Gonzalo, Pedro Ponce, and his cousin, Gonzalo González, Tello Alfonso and his brother Alfonso Téllez.[4]

After discussing what ought to be done, the king, led by the counsel of the Holy Spirit, opted to cross the river Betis [the Guadalquivir], knowing that the Moors of Córdoba could freely cross the bridge to obtain what they needed to fortify the city with food, arms, and men, if necessary. Thus, crossing the river by the bridge which is two leagues beyond Córdoba toward Andújar, he fixed his tents in the area next to the city bridge, that is, between Córdoba and Écija, a city

---

[1] Revelation 4:8: "Day and night they do not stop exclaiming"; Isaiah 62:6: "Never, by day or by night, shall they be silent" (quoted above, chap. 17, n. 1).

[2] 1 Maccabees 10:55: "Happy the day on which you returned to the land of your fathers" (quoted above, chap. 17, n. 10).

[3] These personages were Álvar Pérez de Castro, Bishop Gonzalo of Cuenca, and Bishop Domingo of Baeza.

[4] Infante Alfonso was lord of Molina (see chap. 41). The others were Rodrigo Fernández de Cabrera el feo, Gil Manrique de Manzanedo, Álvar Fernández de Lara, Diego González de Lara, Pedro Ponce de León and his cousin, Gonzalo González, Tello Alfonso de Meneses and Alfonso Téllez de Meneses.

that is only nine leagues distant from Córdoba.[5] When he heard this, Ibn Hûd, the king of the Moors, who was in the region of Murcia, was disturbed and touched inwardly with sorrow in his heart.[6] Gathering a host of four or five thousand knights and a multitude of thirty thousand chosen foot soldiers, he came rapidly to Écija. Also with Ibn Hûd were almost two hundred noble Christian knights who served him for their stipends.[7]

Everyone expected that King Ibn Hûd, trusting in such a great host, would fight to deliver the city of Córdoba from our lord the king. At that time he had with him beyond the bridge only two hundred noble knights and a few others, because Álvar Pérez and certain other knights and all the rest of the people had remained in that part of the city that they held; and they could not cross the river to that area even if they wished to come to the king's aid.

Then the Lord Jesus Christ, the God of the Christians, showered his mercy on those who feared him;[8] and He who had inflamed the heart of the king to come to Córdoba to succor his people, comforted his spirit and those who were with him, and who had placed their souls in his hands.[9] Every day that Ibn Hûd remained at Écija, that is, for fifteen days at least, they expected that the king would come to do battle with them. The Moors and the people of Córdoba awaited him every day.

---

[5] A league was about three to four miles. The bridge was probably at Alcolea, about ten miles east of Córdoba. Andújar is about forty miles east of Córdoba on the Guadalquivir river. The king then eatablished his camp south of the city. Écija is about thirty miles southeast of Córdoba.

[6] Genesis 6:6: "When the Lord saw how great was man's wickedness on earth . . . his heart was grieved" (quoted above, chap. 4, n. 1; chap. 12, n. 5; chap. 19, n. 6; chap. 38, n. 2).

[7] The figures given are clearly exaggerated. On Christians serving as mercenaries in Muslim armies in Spain and Morocco see Charles–Emmanuel Dufourcq, "Les relations du Maroc et de la Castille pendant la première moitié du XIIIe siècle," in idem, L'Ibérie chrétienne et la Maghreb. XIIe–XVe Siècles (Aldershot: Ashgate/Variorum, 1990), no. V:40–45.

[8] Luke 1:50 (from the Magnificat): "His mercy is from age to age to those who fear him." Cf. Psalm 102(103):11.

[9] Luke 23:46: "Father, into your hands I commend my spirit."

72. NEGOTIATIONS FOR THE SURRENDER OF CÓRDOBA

But our Savior, who does not abandon those who hope in Him,[1] confused the counsel of the Moors and crippled their minds and their strength, and they did not dare to engage our glorious king. God, for whom it is equally easy to triumph with a few or with many,[2] was with him. Our king and his army suffered again from a great want of food, and rain without ceasing, and rivers and streams flooding beyond measure.

The king of the Moors mentioned above went to Seville with a certain part of his army, dismissing the rest of the host; feigning certain vain and false reasons, on that account he withdrew to Écija. The heart of Córdoba withered in its very being.[3] Seeing what had happened and knowing that their king did not dare to engage our lord the king, and despairing of outside aid, they intended to resist until death.

After Easter, however, the Castilian militias arrived.[4] Then the Leonese and the Galicians followed them. The people of certain towns, namely those of Salamanca, Zamora, and Toro, had come before them. Knowing that food was lacking in the city, the Christians blockaded the roads and rivers on the order of the lord king and established a siege so that no one could leave or enter.

Then the Moors began to negotiate the surrender of the city, on the condition that they should be allowed to leave, saving their persons and the movable goods that they could carry with them. The king agreed to that condition, but when they had to confirm the pact the Moors held back, thinking that victuals for the army were running out, and that the towns of the kingdom of León did not wish to remain longer, because they had fulfilled three months' [service] in the expedition. But our king, as though he were mocked by King Ibn Hûd, made an alliance with the king of Jaén, who was an enemy of King Ibn Hûd and the Moors of Córdoba. When Ibn Hûd and the Córdobans saw that, they were deeply afraid,

---

[1] Daniel 13:60: "The whole assembly cried aloud, blessing God who saves those who hope in him." Compare the final phrase of the *Te Deum*, sung to celebrate victories: "In te, Domine, speravi: non confundar in aeternum."

[2] Again 1 Samuel (1 Kings) 14:6: "It is no more difficult for the Lord to grant victory through a few than through many" (quoted above, chap. 30, n. 11 and chap. 55, n. 5).

[3] Isaiah 21:4: "My mind reels, shuddering assails me." Cf. Lamentations 2:11: "Worn out from weeping are my eyes, within me all is in ferment."

[4] Easter Sunday was 30 March 1236.

and turned again to our king offering the city to him under the condition already mentioned.[5]

---

[5] Muhammad ibn Nasr, known as Ibn al-Ahmar (1232–1273), founder of the Nasrid dynasty and the kingdom of Granada, which lasted until 1492, had risen in revolt against Ibn Hûd at Arjona in 1232 and was quickly acclaimed by the Moors of Jaén. His alliance with Fernando III helped to hasten the surrender of Córdoba and the downfall of Ibn Hûd. See O'Callaghan, *Medieval Spain,* 343–345.

73. THE CHRISTIANS TAKE POSSESSION OF CÓRDOBA

There were some magnates of the lord king who advised him not to accept that condition, but to take them by force and decapitate them; he could do that because they completely lacked food and, dying of hunger, they were unable to defend the city. On the contrary, the king was persuaded to accept the condition and not to concern himself with the persons of the Moors and their movable goods so long as he could have the city whole and intact.

Indeed, it was known almost for certain that the Córdobans had agreed that if our King Lord Fernando did not wish to accept that condition, they, despairing of life, would destroy everything of value in the city, that is, the mosque and the bridge; they would hide gold and silver; they would cast into the fire silken cloth[1] and indeed the whole city, and would give themselves up to death.

The king accepted the wiser counsel and, on the wish of the king of Jaén, with whom he had made an alliance against King Ibn Hûd and the Córdobans, accepted the condition mentioned before. A pact was concluded under that condition; a truce was granted and established with Ibn Hûd and his subjects for six years, provided, however, that Ibn Hûd paid the king of Castile every third of the year 40,000 and 12,000 *maravedís*. The king of Jaén would receive a certain part of that sum.[2]

With that discussed and settled, the Moors of Córdoba, frustrated in the hope that they had conceived of holding their city, weakened by hunger, left their homes weeping and moaning and groaning out of distress of spirit. Thus by the power of our Lord Jesus Christ, the famous city of Córdoba, endowed with a certain special splendor and rich soil, which had been held captive for such a long time, that is, from the time of Rodrigo, the king of the Goths, was restored to the Christian faith by the labor and valor of our King Lord Fernando.[3]

As the Saracens left he city and fell in droves from hunger, their leader, named Abû-l-Hasan, handed over the keys of the city to our lord the king. Immediately the lord king, as a Catholic man, gave thanks to our Savior, through whose special mercy he recognized that he had received such a great grace in the acquisition of

---

[1] A chief product of Córdoban industry.

[2] Ibn al-Ahmar, the king of Jaén, was Fernando III's ally against Ibn Hûd. The total tribute owed by Ibn Hûd would amount to 156,000 *maravedís* each year. The sum of 12,000 *maravedís* (36,000 annually) probably would be paid to Ibn al-Ahmar.

[3] After defeating the Gothic King Rodrigo in July 711, the Muslims had occupied Córdoba in October of that year. See Collins, *The Arab Conquest of Spain,* 42.

such a noble city. He ordered the standard of the cross to precede his standard and to be placed on the highest tower of the mosque, so that it could wave before his standard in the sight of everyone. Thus when the standard of the eternal king, accompanied by the standard of King Fernando, first appeared on the tower, it caused ineffable confusion and sorrow among the Saracens, and on the other hand, it was seen with ineffable joy by the Christians. That happy day,[4] the happy feast of the Apostles Peter and Paul [29 June 1236], shone for Christians in all the corners of the world; that annual solemnity was celebrated that day.

Around vespers, the chancellor, that is, the bishop of Osma, together with Master Lope, who had first placed the standard of the cross on the tower, entered the mosque and prepared those things that were necessary so that the mosque could be transformed into a church. Eradicating the superstition and filthiness of Muhammad, they sanctified the place by sprinkling holy water with salt, and what had once been the devil's lair was made a church of Jesus Christ, named in honor of his glorious Mother.[5]

On the next day, Monday, the lord king with his barons and with all the people entered the city and went to the church, where he was received honorably with a solemn procession by the bishop of Osma and by the bishops of Cuenca and Baeza and religious men who were then present and by all the clergy.[6]

---

[4] Again 1 Maccabees 10:55: "Happy the day on which you returned to the land of your fathers" (quoted above, chap. 17, n. 10 and chap. 71, n. 2).

[5] The royal chancellor, Bishop Juan of Osma, the probable author of our *Chronicle*, and Master Lope of Fitero consecrated the mosque as a church dedicated to the Virgin Mary. Master Lope was later consecrated as the bishop of Córdoba. The mosque served the Christians until the sixteenth century when a church in the Renaissance style was constructed in its very center. On the ritual for purifying the mosque see above, chap. 50, n. 3.

[6] The king's solemn entrance into Córdoba took place on 30 June 1236. The bishops were Juan of Osma, Gonzalo of Cuenca, and Domingo of Baeza.

74. PROVISION FOR THE DEFENSE AND SETTLEMENT
OF CÓRDOBA

After mass was celebrated solemnly by the bishop of Osma and benediction given to the people, the lord king entered the most noble palace that the kings of the Moors had prepared for themselves. So much and so many wonderful things were said about it by those who saw it, that those who had not seen it found it unbelievable. Thus, there was great joy that day in that city.

The barons and powerful men who served the lord king in the siege and entered the city with him were these: Álvar Pérez and the others named above, who had come to Córdoba with the king. Some of them, however, on the king's command, had returned to obtain the knights with whom they were bound to serve the king. Those who had come from Castile after Easter were these: García Fernández with his sons-in-law and his sons; Diego López and his brother Alfonso López; Rodrigo González; from the kingdom of León and Galicia: Ramiro Froilaz and his brother, Rodrigo Froilaz; Rodrigo Gómez and Fernando Gutiérrez; Fernando Yáñez and Pelayo Arias; from Asturias: Ordoño Álvarez, Pelayo Pérez, and Sebastián Gutiérrez.[1]

Thus the celebrated king sat on the throne of glory of the kingdom of Córdoba, and began to treat with his barons about what needed to be done and how to provide for such a great city, which, after the sudden evacuation of the Moorish people, had to be populated by new inhabitants, followers of Christ. The walls remained standing; the sublime height of the walls was adorned with lofty towers; the houses were resplendent with gilded paneling;[2] the streets of the city, arranged in order, lie open to passersby; but despite the great glory of the city, few were found who wished to remain there. The magnates, lacking food and money, and feeling weary from their long stay, were in a hurry to return home. But the noble king quietly turned over in his mind various outcomes; and after different counsels of the barons, he chose to remain there with a few people. Rather than leave such a noble city, taken with such great exertion, without a governor to defend it and reside there, he submitted himself to the divine will.

At last it was arranged thus: each of the magnates and masters of the orders

---

[1] The Castilians were García Fernández de Villamayor, Diego and Alfonso López de Haro, and Rodrigo González Girón. The Leonese were Ramiro and Rodrigo Froilaz, sons of Count Froyla; Rodrigo Gómez de Trastámara; Fernando Yáñez de Limia; and Ordoño Álvarez de Asturias. The others cannot be identified more precisely.

[2] Cf. Virgil, *Aeneid*, 1:726: *laquearibus aureis*.

would leave knights there with arms and horses; other warlike men would also remain with them. At that time one hundred and fifty knights from Segovia, equipped with arms and horses and abundant food, arrived. The lord king, moreover, appointed over all those who remained in the city Tello Alfonso; his brother Alfonso Téllez remained with him. Skillful in arms, both young men[3] were prepared to die and to defend the city.

With that arranged, the lord king with his barons returned to Toledo to his mother. There he was received with much honor and great joy. Extending his stay there, around the beginning of the month of August he fell sick in bed, and remained there for a long time; he scarcely escaped the danger of death.

Around the feast of St. Michael [29 September], while the king continued to stay in Toledo because of his serious weakness, such a great host of people, quite suddenly and unexpectedly, rushed to Córdoba, so that the ancient house hardly sufficed for its new inhabitants. Thus divine providence relieved what the great council feared.[4]

---

[3] Tello Alfonso and Alfonso Téllez de Meneses.

[4] The "great council" (*magnum consilium*) was the royal court.

75. FERNANDO III LEAVES TOLEDO FOR BURGOS

Then on the feast of St. Luke [18 October] Lope Díaz, a powerful and rich man, went the way of all flesh. When he heard this the lord king and his mother, as soon as he was able to ride, left Toledo and arrived at Burgos at the end of the month of November.[1]

I finished this work in, I think, a short time.[2]

Praise be to you, O Christ.[3]

---

[1] The king was in Toledo at least until 28 October 1236.

[2] The colophon, "Hoc opus expleui, tempore, credo, breui" is a dactylic pentameter, followed by the liturgical cadence, "Laus, tibi, Christe."

[3] These may be the words of the copyist, rather than the author.

Select Bibliography

SOURCES

Chronica latina regum Castellae. In *Chronica Hispana Saeculi XIII*. Ed. Luis Charlo Brea, Juan A. Estévez Soila, and Rocío Carande Herrera. *Corpus Christianorum. Continuatio Mediaevalis* 73. Turnhout: Brepols, 1997. 9–118.

Chronique latine des rois de Castille jusqu'en 1236. Ed. Georges Cirot. Bordeaux: Feret et Fils, 1913.

Cirot, Georges, ed. "Une chronique latine inédite des rois de Castille jusqu'en 1236." *Bulletin Hispanique* 14 (1912): 30–46, 109–118, 244–274, 353–374; 15 (1913): 18–37, 170–187, 268–283, 411–427.

———. "Une chronique latine inédite des rois de Castille jusqu' en 1236." *Bulletin Hispanique* 22 (1920): 1–153.

Crónica latina de los reyes de Castilla. Ed. María Desamparados Cabanes Pecourt. Valencia: Anubar, 1964.

Crónica latina de la reyes de Castilla. Ed. Luis Charlo Brea. Cádiz: Universidad de Cádiz, 1984.

Crónica latina de los reyes de Castilla. Trans. Luis Charlo Brea. Madrid: Akal, 1999.

De expugnatione Lyxbonensi. The Conquest of Lisbon. Ed. and trans. Charles W. David. New York: Columbia University Press, 1936.

Diego García. *Planeta*. Ed. Manuel Alonso. Madrid: Consejo superior de Investigaciones científicas, 1943.

Les registres de Grégoire IX. Ed. Lucien Auvray. 2 vols. Paris: Bibliothèque des Ecoles françaises d'Athènes et de Rome, 1896–1955.

Lucas of Túy. *Chronicon mundi*. Ed. Andreas Schott. *Hispania Illustrata*. 4 vols. Frankfort: Claudius Marnius et Heredes Joannis Aubrii, 1603–1608. 4:1–116.

———. *Crónica de España*. Ed. and trans. Julio Puyol. Madrid: Revista de Archivos, Bibliotecas y Museos, 1926.

Poema de Fernán González. Ed. Alonso Zamora Vicente. Clásicos Castellanos. Madrid: Espasa-Calpe, 1946.

Rodrigo Jiménez de Rada. *Historia de rebus Hispanie sive Historia Gothica*. Ed. Juan Fernández Valverde. *Corpus Christianorum. Continuatio Mediaevalis 72*. Turnhout: Brepols, 1987.

The Chronicle of James I, King of Aragon. Trans. J. Forster. 2 vols. London: Chapman and Hall, 1883.

The Chronicle of San Juan de la Peña. A Fourteenth-Century Official History of the Crown of Aragon. Trans. Lynn H. Nelson. Philadelphia: University of Pennsylvania Press, 1991.

The Code of Cuenca. Municipal Law on the Twelfth-Century Castilian Frontier. Trans. James F. Powers. Philadelphia: University of Pennsylvania Press, 2000.

MODERN WORKS

Abulafia, David. *Frederick II. A Medieval Emperor*. Oxford: Oxford University Press, 1992.

Angold, M.J. "John of Brienne." *Oxford Dictionary of Byzantium (ODB)*. 3 vols. New York: Oxford University Press, 1991. 2:1062–1063.

Baer, Yitzhak. *A History of the Jews in Christian Spain*. 2 vols. Philadelphia: Jewish Publication Society, 1966.

Ballesteros, Antonio. *Alfonso X, el Sabio*. Barcelona, 1963; Reprint Barcelona: El Albir, 1984.

Barton, Simon. *The Aristocracy in Twelfth-Century León and Castile*. Cambridge: Cambridge University Press, 1997.

Bisson, Thomas N. *The Medieval Crown of Aragon. A Short History*. Oxford: Clarendon Press, 1986.

Brand, Charles M. *Byzantium Confronts the West, 1180–1204*. Cambridge, Mass.: Harvard University Press, 1968. 2d ed. Aldershot: Gregg, 1992.

——. "Alexios IV Angelos." *ODB* 1:65–66.

——. "Alexios V Doukas." *ODB* 1:66.

——. "Baldwin of Flanders." *ODB* 1:247–248.

——. "Boniface of Montferrat." *ODB* 1:304–305.

——. "Frederick I Barbarossa." *ODB*. 2:804.

——. "Isaac II Angelos." *ODB* 2:1012.

——. "Philip of Swabia." *ODB* 3:1653.

Burns, Robert I., S.J. "The Spiritual Life of James the Conqueror, King of

Arago-Catalonia, 1208–1276: Portrait and Self Portrait." *Catholic Historical Review* 62 (1976): 1–35.

Charlo Brea, Luis. "¿Un segundo autor para la última parte de la *Crónica latina de los reyes de Castilla?*" *Actas del I Congreso Nacional de Latín Medieval (León, 1–4 diciembre de 1993).* León: Universidad de León, 1995. 251–256.

Cirot Georges. "Appendices à la Chronique latine des Rois de Castille." *Bulletin Hispanique* 17 (1915): 101–115, 243–258; 20 (1918): 27–35, 149–184; 21 (1919): 173–192.

———. "Recherches sur la Chronique latine des Rois de Castille." *Bulletin Hispanique* 21 (1919): 193–217, 276–281; 25 (1923): 97–107.

Collins, Roger. *Early Medieval Spain. Unity in Diversity, 400–1000.* New York: St. Martin's Press, 1983.

———. *The Arab Conquest of Spain, 710–797.* Oxford: Blackwell, 1994.

Donovan, Joseph P. *Pelagius and the Fifth Crusade.* Philadelphia: University of Pennsylvania Press, 1950.

Dufourcq, Charles-Emmanuel. "Les relations du Maroc et de la Castille pendant la première moitié du XIIIe siècle." In idem, *L'Ibérie chrétienne et la Maghreb. XIIe–XVe Siècles* (Aldershot, Hampshire: Ashgate/Variorum, 1990). No. V.

Fernández Martín, Pedro. "El Obispo de Osma, canciller de Fernando III el Santo, no se llamaba Juan Domínguez." *Celtiberia* 27 (1964): 79–95.

Fletcher, Richard. *Moorish Spain.* Berkeley: University of California Press, 1992.

Forey, Alan. "The Order of Mountjoy." *Speculum* 46 (1971): 250–266.

González, Julio. *Alfonso IX.* 2 vols. Madrid: Consejo superior de Investigaciones científicas, 1945.

———. *El reino de Castilla en la época de Alfonso VIII.* 3 vols. Madrid: Consejo superior de Investigacions científicas, 1960.

———. *Regesta de Fernando II.* Madrid: Consejo superior de Investigaciones científicas, 1943.

———. *Reinado y diplomas de Fernando III.* 3 vols. Córdoba: Monte de Piedad y Caja de Ahorros, 1980–1986.

———. "La Crónica latina de los Reyes de Castilla." *Homenaje a don Agustín Millares Carlo.* 2 vols. Palma: Caja Insular de Ahorros de Gran Canaria, 1975. 2:55–70.

Hallam, Elizabeth M. *Capetian France, 987–1328.* London and New York: Longman, 1980.

Harvey, L. P. *Islamic Spain, 1250 to 1500*. Chicago: University of Chicago Press, 1990.

Huici Miranda, Ambrosio. *Las grandes batallas de la reconquista*. Madrid: Consejo superior de Investigaciones científicas, 1956.

Hussey, Joan M. *The Byzantine World*. New York: Harper, 1961.

Kazhdan, Alexander. "Innocent III." *ODB* 2:996.

———. "Thomas Morosini." *ODB* 3:2077.

Kennedy, Hugh. *Muslim Spain and Portugal. A Political History of al-Andalus*. London and New York: Longman, 1996.

Linehan, Peter. *History and the Historians of Medieval Spain*. Oxford: Clarendon Press, 1993.

———. *The Spanish Church and the Papacy in the Thirteenth Century*. Cambridge: Cambridge University Press, 1971.

Livermore, Harold V. *A New History of Portugal*. Cambridge: Cambridge University Press, 1966.

Lomax, Derek W. *The Reconquest of Spain*. London and New York: Longman, 1978.

———. "The Authorship of the *Chronique latine des rois de Castille*." *Bulletin of Hispanic Studies* 40 (1963): 205–211.

Lourie, Elena. *Crusade and Colonisation. Muslims, Christians and Jews in Medieval Aragon*. London: Variorum, 1990.

———. "The Will of Alfonso I 'el Batallador,' King of Aragon and Navarre: A Reassessment" *Speculum* 50 (1975): 635–651. Reproduced in eadem, *Crusade and Colonisation*. No. III.

———. "The Will of Alfonso I of Aragon and Navarre: A Reply to Dr. Forey." *Durham University Journal* 77 (1984–85): 165–172. Reproduced in eadem, *Crusade and Colonisation*. No. IV.

MacKay, Angus. *Spain in the Middle Ages. From Frontier to Empire, 1000–1500*. New York: St. Martin's Press, 1983.

Márquez Sterling, Manuel. *Fernán González. The Man and the Legend*. Oxford: University of Mississippi, 1980.

Millares Carlo, Agustín. "La cancillería real en León y Castilla hasta fines del reinado de Fernando III." *Anuario de Historia del Derecho Español* 3 (1926): 227–306.

O'Callaghan, Joseph F. *A History of Medieval Spain*. Ithaca: Cornell University Press, 1975.

———. *Alfonso X, The Cortes, and Government in Medieval Spain.* Aldershot, Hampshire: Ashgate/Variorum, 1998.

———. *The Spanish Military Order of Calatrava and its Affiliates.* London: Variorum, 1975).

———. "The Beginnings of the Cortes of León-Castile." *American Historical Review* 74 (1969): 1503–1537. Reproduced in idem, *Alfonso X, The Cortes, and Government in Medieval Spain.* No. IX.

———. "The Foundation of the Order of Alcántara, 1176–1218." *Catholic Historical Review* 47 (1962): 471–486. Reproduced in idem, *The Spanish Military Order of Calatrava and its Affiliates.* No. IV.

———. "The Order of Calatrava, 1158–1212: Years of Crisis and Survival." In Vladimir P. Goss and Christine Verzár Bornstein, ed. *The Meeting of Two Worlds. Cultural Exchange between East and West during the Period of the Crusades.* Kalamazoo: Western Michigan University Press, 1986. 419–430.

———. "Innocent III and the Kingdoms of Castile and León." In John C. Moore, ed. *Pope Innocent III and his World.* Aldershot: Ashgate, 1999. 317–335.

Oliveira Marques, A. H. de. *History of Portugal.* 2 vols. 2d. ed. New York: Columbia University Press, 1976.

Pérez de Urbel, Justo. *Sancho el Mayor de Navarra.* Madrid: Consejo superior de Investigaciones científicas, 1950.

Post, Gaines. *Studies in Medieval Legal Thought. Public Law and the State, 1100–1322.* Princeton: Princeton University Press, 1964.

Powers, James F. *A Society Organized for War. The Iberian Municipal Militias in the Central Middle Ages, 1000–1284.* Berkeley: University of California Press, 1988.

Queller, Donald E., and T. E. Madden. *The Fourth Crusade. The Conquest of Constantinople, 1201–1204.* 2d ed. Philadelphia: University of Pennsylvania Press, 1997.

Reilly, Bernard F. *The Contest of Christian and Muslim Spain, 1031–1157.* Oxford: Blackwell, 1992.

———. *The Kingdom of León-Castilla under King Alfonso VI, 1065–1109.* Princeton: Princeton University Press, 1988.

———. *The Kingdom of León-Castilla under King Alfonso VII, 1126–1157.* Philadelphia: University of Pennsylvania Press, 1998.

———. *The Kingdom of León-Castilla under Queen Urraca, 1109–1126.* Princeton: Princeton University Press, 1982.

Riley-Smith, Jonathan. *The Crusades. A Short History.* New Haven: Yale University Press, 1987.

Rivera Recio, Juan Francisco. "Personajes hispanos asistentes en 1215 al IV Concilio de Letrán." *Hispania Sacra* 4 (1951): 335–355.

Sánchez Alonso, Benito. *Historia de la historiografía española.* 2 vols. Madrid: Consejo superior de Investigaciones científicas, 1941–1944.

———. *Fuentes de la historia española e hispano-americana.* 3d ed. Madrid: Revista de Filología española, 1952.

Serrano, Luciano. "El canciller de Fernando III de Castilla." *Hispania* (1941): 3–40.

Vallvé, Joaquín. "Sobre algunas problemas de la invasión musulmana." *Anuario de Estudios Medievales* 4 (1967): 361–367.

Wasserstein, David. *The Rise and Fall of the Party Kings, 1002–1086.* Princeton: Princeton University Press, 1985.

Watt, W. Montgomery. *A History of Islamic Spain.* Edinburgh: University Press, 1965.